Finding Our Fulfillment in Christ

Finding Our Fulfillment in Christ: A Lent Devotional Study for Women

Copyright 2020 © Rebekah Hargraves

REBEKAH HARGRAVES

Finding Our Fulfillment in Christ

A Lent Devotional Study for Women

Dedicated to my dear, kindred spirit friends,
Tina and Jessica,
who never stop reminding me that my worth
is not found in what I do, but in Christ, and that
I must rest and refresh before I can minister and pour out.

I love you both to the moon and back and don't know where I would
be without our Thursday Bible studies, Friday night Hallmark movie
marathons,
and Saturday morning coffee dates.

This book is for you.

Table of Contents

Part 2: The Path to the Cross

Introduction

I grew up (and still remain) a member of the Baptist church. And while my twenty-seven-years-long stint as a Baptist has included time spent in Southern Baptist, Reformed Baptist, and even Independent Fundamental Baptist churches, one thing remained the same: I had no clue what Lent was for more than two decades of my life.

I do have one memory as a child of going with my Grams to an Ash Wednesday church service and having ashes applied to my forehead, but I didn't know why or what it was for. As I got older and grew deeper in my understanding of Protestantism, the Catholic Church, and church history, I began to assume that Lent was solely a Catholic thing and merely a season of penance. To my Protestant, Five Solas-believing mind, I had no use for any season of penance. To me, penance meant trying to absolve yourself of the wrongs you have committed and, therefore, was contradictory to the truth of the gospel. I certainly didn't want anything to do with a forty-day Lenten season of fasting from anything, because that felt like a system of works to me (never mind the fact that fasting and prayer are mentioned in conjunction with one another throughout the four gospels and on into the rest of the New Testament!). To me, Lent was nothing more than a time of depriving and beating yourself over your sin. And I didn't see a call for that in the "plan of salvation."

As convinced as I was that I knew what the forty-day season of Lent was all about (which is funny to me now, considering I had never taken the time to study it specifically), I discovered over the past couple of years that I was wrong. My journey into studying, learning about, and understanding the traditional "church calendar" began in 2015 when I heard the term "Advent" for the first time and absolutely fell in love with that four-week period. I have celebrated and commemorated the season of Advent every year since, always looking forward to it more and more with each passing Christmas. In the summer of 2018 I even wrote an Advent devotional study for women.

To coincide beautifully with the writing of that Advent study, I was also learning more about the season of Lent. In fact, my study of Lent has continued until just a few weeks ago, and I am happy to be putting what I have learned into book form to present to you—just as I did with the Advent study.

In the same way that Advent leads up to and makes the Christmas season infinitely more special and meaningful, my prayer is that, through the pages of this devotional study, commemorating the forty days leading up to Resurrection Sunday would do the same for your Easter celebration as well.

While I used to think Lent was about deprivation, penance, and sackcloth and ashes, what I have come to discover is that the opposite is true: It really is a season that shifts our focus—not onto ourselves, but onto the gospel of Christ! As Joan Chittister wrote in her book *The Liturgical Year: The Spiraling Adventure of the Spiritual Life,*

> Each succeeding year, Lent calls each of us to renew our ongoing commitment to the implications of the Resurrection in our own lives, here and now. But that demands both the healing and the honing of the soul, both a purging of what is superfluous in our lives and the heightening, the intensifying, of what is meaningful. Lent is a call to renew a commitment grown dull, perhaps, by a life marked more by routine than by reflection.[1]

She goes on to say,

> Lent is not a ritual. It is time given to think seriously about Who Jesus is for us, to renew our faith from the inside out....Steeped in the consciousness of the cross of Christ, the Christian goes again to the tomb of the heart, stripped of its distractions and lusts to say, "I believe."[2]

The purpose of Lent is to break into our everyday, busy, distracted, hurried, seemingly mundane lives with the life-changing truth of the gospel. It is to remind us of who we are in Christ, what our calling is in Him, and the fact that we will not find the ultimate fulfillment we are longing for in anything other than Christ—not in marriage, motherhood, work, or even ministry. No, our identity, our fulfillment,

1 Joan Chittister, *The Liturgical Year: The Spiraling Adventure of the Spiritual Life* (Nashville, Tennessee: Thomas Nelson, Inc., 2009) pg. 110-111
2 Ibid, pg. 111

our purpose, and our longings can only be met in the person and work of Jesus Christ, and that is something of which we need to be reminded regularly.

So, over the next forty days of this Lenten season, will you come away with me? Come away from the distractions, the busyness, and the hustle and bustle of the everyday and purpose in your heart to fast from one thing (maybe it will be social media, a certain kind of food, something that is overextending your schedule but which you think you "have" to do, a drink that has become an idol, etc.) so that you can instead fix your gaze on something else (the gospel and its implications for your everyday life).

The journey you are about to begin will be divided between two main topics of study. The first thirty-three days will be a survey of thirty-three women of the Bible who were tempted to seek fulfillment and satisfaction in the things of this world but who ultimately found them in God and His truth. We will learn from these women, be inspired by these women, and perhaps even feel sorry for some of these women. Along the way, we will discover them to be sisters of ours whose lives were ultimately changed by our great God. As we study them, may we be inspired to turn a blind eye to the wooing of the world that we might fix our gaze on Christ instead.

The second portion of the study, the final seven days leading up to Resurrection Sunday, will consist of a study of Christ—His life, passion week, His death, and, finally, His resurrection. The result of which will be our coming to understand perhaps more fully than ever before just how meaningful the reality of Easter is for our everyday lives.

May you walk away from this study at the end of the forty days of Lent feeling more love, adoration, and thanksgiving toward Christ and His work on your behalf than ever before. And may your life be forever changed as a result.

Your sister in the journey,
Rebekah Hargraves

Part I

The Path to Fulfillment

Day 1

Eve and the Quest for Knowledge

Then the serpent said to the woman, "You will not surely die. For God knows that in the day you eat of it your eyes will be opened, and you will be like God, knowing good and evil." So when the woman saw that the tree was good for food, that it was pleasant to the eyes, and a tree desirable to make one wise, she took of its fruit and ate."

—Genesis 3:4-6a

Wisdom is the right use of knowledge. To know is not to be wise. Many men know a great deal, and are all the greater fools for it. There is no fool so great a fool as a knowing fool, but to know how to use knowledge is to have wisdom.

—Charles Haddon Spurgeon[1]

From our perspective now in this fallen and sin-cursed world, it would appear that Eve easily had everything she could have ever wanted: a beautiful home, a loving husband, a caring and present God, and no pain, death, destruction, or heartache. Eve, however, wasn't quite so convinced. She wanted more.

From the moment the serpent first appeared on the scene to tempt her, Eve began to feel a rumbling within herself that she perhaps had never felt before—a longing, an idea that maybe she was missing out on something, even here, even now, in the midst of such a lush and beautiful garden.

---

1 http://christian-quotes.ochristian.com/christian-quotes_ochristian.cgi?find=Christian-quotes-by-Charles+Spurgeon-on-Knowledge, accessed September 11, 2019

No, the loving husband (there was no marital strife!), the close and intimate relationship with her Creator, and the majestic beauty of her surroundings were not enough. It wasn't enough to simply enjoy what God had given her; she wanted more. She wanted precisely that which God had not seen fit to give her: the knowledge of not only good, but also evil.

That doesn't quite sound like something you would jump at the chance to acquire, does it? Why not live in peaceful ignorance of evil and enjoy your life in paradise, Eve? And yet, we do the very same thing ourselves when we turn our eyes, our minds, and our hearts to those darker things which we, especially as believers, have no business becoming involved in. Eve's problem was that she was not willing to remain the creation; she wanted to become as the Creator.

This desire is not to be confused with our legitimate, God-given mission to be image bearers of God and, as Christians, ambassadors of Christ; it is different. Eve's desire in that moment of temptation that led to her subsequent sin was to possess all the wisdom and knowledge (and, therefore, the resulting power) of God. Being in a relationship with Him as His child wasn't what she wanted. She wanted to *be* Him.

You may be wondering how this applies to us today and what this has to do with the season of Lent. Well, as we saw in the introduction, the forty-day season of Lent is designed to prepare our hearts to truly grasp, remember, and celebrate the full meaning of Easter. This is accomplished by purposefully clearing away the distractions which so easily divert our attention and keep us from meditating on the truths of the gospel.

For many of us (including myself), these distractions are related to social media. We may be addicted to scrolling Instagram or Facebook so that we can see what is going on in other people's lives. We can't seem to get away from Twitter because we have become addicted to acquiring the knowledge of what are the opinions of others on issues pertaining to politics, theology, and issues among church leaders. Maybe your daily downfall is Google and the incessant search to discover what all the "experts" have to say about the seemingly best parenting, schooling, feeding, disciplining, and home management methods.

Though the heart motivation may be different, the end result is the same: We are daily doing exactly that for which we commonly criticize Eve. We look at her and wonder why she thought she needed more. And yet, here we are, with the words of God bound together in one complete volume that we have moment-by-moment access to, and yet we are exchanging that incredible privilege and gift (which many of our brothers and sisters around the world are seeing fall through their fingertips) for the words and "wisdom" of man. We have all the wisdom, knowledge, and answers we could ever need within the pages of the Bible, and yet we leave it sitting dusty on the shelf so that we can spend all our time scrolling through the thoughts of fallible humans. In our quest for knowledge, we have become fools. We have exchanged the eternal for the temporal.

But you know what? There is good news! There is no condemnation for those who are in Christ (Romans 8:1). Don't wallow in guilt over misplaced priorities or a vain search for man-made knowledge. Instead, get up, dust yourself (and your Bible, if needed!) off, and begin anew, right where you are. Make it your aim over the next forty days to get into the Word however and wherever you need to. Perhaps you will need to take advantage of the audio option available through the YouVersion Bible App so that you can listen on the go, or maybe you will be in the Word during your lunch break or while your kids watch a little show. Even if it is just for five minutes a day, it counts and is worth it!

God promises us that His Word will not return void (Isaiah 55:11), that it is alive, active, and more powerful than any two-edged sword (Hebrews 4:12). The power of the knowledge of God and His Word in your life is not dependent upon the atmosphere surrounding your quiet (or not so quiet!) time. It is dependent on simply getting into the Word itself. I encourage you to do just that over the next forty days and, thereby, begin a habit that will serve you well throughout the rest of your life. And if you think you just don't have the time? Instead of opening the Instagram, Twitter, or Facebook app when you usually would, open up the Bible app instead, and you'll discover just how much time you truly do have!

Action Step:

Change your life for the better and increase your knowledge of those things which truly matter by getting into the Word today. Even if just for five minutes, get into the Word and allow the Word to get into you.

Prayer:

"Lord, today and over the next forty days, help me desire to be in the Word. So often it is more fun and enticing to scroll social media or watch Netflix to unwind, when really what would ultimately nourish me—body, mind, and soul—is Your Word. Help me to remember that and hunger and thirst for it as You intended. Help me to remember that man's knowledge is nothing compared to Yours, and use that to drive me daily into Your Word and Your truth. Guide and direct me, Lord, and change me through this journey. In Jesus' name, Amen."

Day 2

Sarah and the Quest for a Legacy and a Promise

Now Sarai, Abram's wife, had borne him no children. And she had an Egyptian maidservant whose name was Hagar. So Sarai said to Abram, "See now, the Lord has restrained me from bearing children. Please, go in to my maid; perhaps I shall obtain children by her." And Abram heeded the voice of Sarai.

—Genesis 16:1-2

The will of God is never exactly what you expect it to be. It may seem to be much worse, but in the end it's going to be a lot better and a lot bigger.

—Elisabeth Elliot[1]

I have often read, in utter astonishment, the account in Genesis 16 of Sarah giving her maidservant to her husband. *What was she thinking? How could she possibly be okay with her husband sleeping with another woman? She's willing to have her husband father another woman's child? What in the world is wrong with her?*

Before we jump too quickly to thinking Sarah may have needed a mental evaluation, there is something important to note: It wasn't so much that there was something wrong with Sarah, as it was that there was something terribly wrong with the culture in which she was living.

1 http://christian-quotes.ochristian.com/Patience-Quotes/page-5.shtml, accessed September 12, 2019

You see, the severely patriarchal culture which served as a backdrop for the story of the Bible (not to be confused with the myth that the Bible itself and God Himself are patriarchal!) taught that a woman's sole purpose was to bear children, thereby furthering her husband's family line. That was the primary way in which women could contribute to society. And if they didn't? Well, they were pretty much viewed as worthless.

You can imagine, then, Sarah's desperation. Here she is, well into her golden years, still childless. She has gone through her whole life believing that she has failed at the one thing she was made to do: have babies. Her husband loves her, but she still feels as if she has let him down. What does she do then? She takes matters into her own hands. After all, four whole chapters earlier, in Genesis 12, God had made the promise to Abraham that he would be made into a great nation. How could that happen apart from descendants?

So, Sarah does what to us feels like the unthinkable and gives her maidservant to her husband so that they might produce an heir for Abraham and help God's hand along a little in His plan to make Abraham into that great nation. The sad part about this? God didn't need any help, and it was Sarah's racing ahead of God, to try to insure on her own that God's promise would come to pass, which led to much of the heartache and turmoil we read in the chapters in Genesis that follow.

What are you hoping for today, friend? What are you wishing for, trying to make happen, working yourself to the bone in order to bring it to pass? What if I were to tell you that you would not be fulfilled even if that legacy or that promise or that goal came to fruition if you don't know Christ? It's true. Consider a few passages of Scripture with me for a moment:

> What profit has a man from all his labor in which he toils under the sun? One generation passes away, and another generation comes; but the earth abides forever.
>
> —Ecclesiastes 1:3-4

> The grass withers, the flower fades, but the word of our God stands forever.
>
> —Isaiah 40:8

You will show me the path of life; in Your presence is fullness of joy; at Your right hand are pleasures forevermore.

—Psalm 16:11

The Lord will guide you continually, and satisfy your soul in drought, and strengthen your bones; you shall be like a watered garden, and like a spring of water, whose waters do not fail.

—Isaiah 58:11

The truth is that as great as are goals and dreams, as wonderful as it is to see God so faithfully fulfill a promise He has made to one of His children (as He does several chapters later in the birth of Abraham and Sarah's son, Isaac), what is far more lasting and fulfilling is being in relationship with God Himself. The Giver truly is far greater than even His most amazing and best gifts.

Leaving behind a wonderful legacy and desiring to see promises of God fulfilled are wonderful goals. But we make a grave mistake when we do as Sarah did and jump ahead of God out of a wrong belief that our God-given legacy will be more fulfilling to us than God Himself.

Whatever your life goals may be in this season, and whatever legacy you may be working toward being able to leave behind, temper that zeal just a bit with the truths of God's Word. Remember that all our work is empty vanity apart from Christ. Remember that walking by the Spirit is what must become our practice if we want to live a truly fruitful, fulfilling life on this earth. And that is only done through Bible study, prayer, and seeking the face of God.

Action Step:

Take a step back from your to-do list today and ask yourself, *Am I finding more joy in what I accomplish, or am I finding more joy in simply being mindful of the moment-by-moment presence of God and the relationship I have with Him?* Spend some time in prayer today over that question and make any necessary changes in your day-to-day life that God may impress upon your heart to make.

Prayer:

Lord, I know I don't always look for and find my fulfillment in You. I clamor over what You can give me more than I simply delight in Who You are and the relationship I can have with You. Change my heart in this area, Lord. Help me to love and delight in You more than any promise, gift, or legacy You could ever give me. Help me to know, believe, and remember that You are the ultimate treasure. In Jesus' name, Amen.

Day 3

Hagar and the Quest for Recognition

Then she called the name of the Lord who spoke to her, You-Are-the-God-Who-Sees; for she said, "Have I also here seen Him who sees me."

—Genesis 16:13

If you have ever been lost in a wilderness, treated unjustly, dealt with harshly, or have fled in fear or in the hope of something better, Hagar's story is for you. It is evidence of God's abiding grace, no matter what. You aren't alone. The Lord sees you. He hears. He knows. He is with you. His grace will comfort you.

—Robin Jones Gunn[1]

As crazy as we may have believed Sarah's actions to be when we studied her story yesterday, just think about the implications for her poor maidservant! Just as patriarchy's teachings led Sarah into a seemingly hopeless situation, Sarah's actions led her maidservant into a hopeless situation as well. As a servant, Hagar was expected to do her mistress Sarah's bidding—even when that meant sleeping with Sarah's husband.

Not only was Hagar forced to obey Sarah's wishes, but things went from bad to worse for her a few verses later:

---

1 https://www.goodreads.com/quotes/search?utf8=%E2%9C%93&q=hagar&commit=Search, accessed September 12, 2019

So he went in to Hagar, and she conceived. And when she saw that she had conceived, her mistress became despised in her eyes. Then Sarai said to Abram, "My wrong be upon you! I gave my maid into your embrace; and when she saw that she had conceived, I became despised in her eyes. The Lord judge between you and me." So Abram said to Sarai, "Indeed your maid is in your hand; do to her as you please." And when Sarai dealt harshly with her, she fled from her presence.

—Genesis 16:4-6

Granted, Hagar should not have entertained such a despised view of Sarah, but what Sarah did in dealing harshly with her put Hagar in a very difficult situation. This difficult time in her life is precisely the moment when God showed up for Hagar like at no other time before. Verses 7-11 say,

Now the Angel of the Lord found her by a spring of water in the wilderness, by the spring on the way to Shur. And He said, "Hagar, Sarai's maid, where have you come from, and where are you going?" She said, "I am fleeing from the presence of my mistress Sarai." The Angel of the Lord said to her, "Return to your mistress, and submit yourself under her hand." Then the Angel of the Lord said to her, "I will multiply your descendants exceedingly, so that they shall not be counted for multitude." And the Angel of the Lord said to her: "Behold, you are with child, and you shall bear a son. You shall call his name Ishmael, because *the Lord has heard your affliction*." (Emphasis my own.)

Are you going through a hard season in your life where you feel like you are all alone and nobody cares, sees, or is even fully aware? Perhaps you are a young mama at home with your little ones, working day after day to care for them, and you feel like no one sees or appreciates your work. Maybe you are going through a dark time with your husband having betrayed you, and you are feeling ignored and rejected, alone in your pain and heartache. Or perhaps you recently lost a dear loved one, someone who always went out of their way to take time to bless and encourage you, and now you feel like you have no one in your life who cares about you and the concerns of your heart.

May I encourage you today? God sees. He cares. And He is with you.

If anyone could understand how you are feeling right now, it would be Hagar. This poor woman felt the same feelings of rejection, loneliness, and misunderstanding that you now may be experiencing.

Hagar did all of Sarah's bidding—even the bidding which seems downright crazy and repulsive to us today. Yet, her obedience to Sarah—what should have led to her finding favor in her mistress's eyes— actually led to Sarah treating her harshly and unfairly. Hagar traveled into the wilderness upon leaving Sarah and was met there by the Angel of the Lord Himself Who comforted her, "heard [her] affliction", and promised to "multiply [her] descendants exceedingly." Verse 13 goes on to say, "Then she called the name of the Lord who spoke to her, You-Are-the-God-Who-Sees." (In Hebrew this is "El Roi," the first name given to God by a human being.)

Friend, take heart and see—the Lord is not unfeeling toward us! Far from it. He loves us deeply, views us tenderly as His daughters, and is always present—even when we are feeling hurt and alone, rejected and unseen.

I recently came across Hebrews 6:10, and it instantly struck me:

> For God is not unjust to forget your work and labor of love which you have shown toward His name, in that you have ministered to the saints, and do minister.

How well that applies to us busy women who are daily tending to the never-ending needs of our children or working to care for our husbands or dedicating time to the upkeep and productivity of our homes! We may feel unseen, forgotten, and unappreciated, but we simply are not. Our Lord sees our faithful work, remembers it, and values it.

The following are some other passages I find encouraging in this area:

> But when you do a charitable deed, do not let your left hand know what your right hand is doing, that your charitable deed may be in secret; and your Father who sees in secret will Himself reward you openly.

—Matthew 6:3-4

Be strong and of good courage, do not fear nor be afraid of them;
for the Lord your God, He is the One who goes with you. He
will not leave you nor forsake you.

—Deuteronomy 31:6

Sweet reader, please know that you are not alone. Whether you are
once again washing a tower of dishes at your kitchen sink or staring
at yet another newly-arrived bill in the mail, wondering how you will
be able to pay it, or reeling from the heartache of some recent tragedy
in your life, He sees you. Right where you are, He sees you. In this very
moment with exactly what you are doing in this day, He sees you. And
He will never look away.

The same is true for you if your story is a bit different from those
stories of hardship faced by our sisters in Christ. Sometimes our quest
for recognition isn't about wishing someone saw our pain, so much as
it is a case of idolatry in our hearts. Sometimes we want to be noticed
on social media, lauded for our wisdom and insight, followed by the
masses, and seen by a multitude of clamoring followers. Even then,
sometimes it is pain that is the driving force behind our quest for
recognition—pain stemming from our wanting to be seen, known,
and loved but not understanding who we are in Christ or how loved,
treasured, and seen we truly already are by the Creator God of the
universe.

During this Lenten season, I would encourage you to step back
from your quest for recognition and fulfillment, remembering instead
who you are in Christ as a result of the gloriously good news of the
gospel we celebrate this time of the year. Delete the social media apps
from your phone, take a bit of a sabbatical from the internet, and let
the idol of public opinion go, exchanging it instead for the soul rest
that is to be found in knowing how much your God loves you.

Action Step:

Prayerfully consider taking a break from social media, whether it's for
a day, a week, or a month. Take back the time you would have been
using to scroll and use it instead to be in the Word or prayer. See if, at
the end of your sabbatical, you don't treasure the recognition of God
far more than you ever did the recognition of man!

Prayer:

Lord, You know how much my heart yearns to be seen, known, recognized, admired, and loved. You also know that it is my practice to seek the fulfillment of these desires in the arena of public opinion and what man thinks of me. Help me not to be unstable in all my ways as a result of double-mindedly wanting to please You and others. Break me free from these bonds of idolatry, refresh my memory in how You feel about me and always will, and help me to walk in light of that truth. In Jesus' name, Amen.

Day 4

Rebekah and the Quest for Her Own Plan

Now Rebekah was listening when Isaac spoke to Esau his son. And Esau went to the field to hunt game and to bring it. So Rebekah spoke to Jacob her son, saying, "Indeed I heard your father speak to Esau your brother, saying, 'Bring me game and make savory food for me, that I may eat it and bless you in the presence of the Lord before my death.' Now therefore, my son, obey my voice according to what I command you. Go now to the flock and bring me from there two choice kids of the goats, and I will make savory food from them for your father, such as he loves. Then you shall take it to your father, that he may eat it, and that he may bless you before his death."

—Genesis 27:5-10

God always gives you what you would have asked for if you knew everything that He knows.

—Tim Keller[1]

I most definitely live up to my old namesake's sin struggle here, I hate to say. I suppose many of us can relate—we want what we want, how we want it, and when we want it. We think we know best, we have our own agenda, and if God doesn't jump to make it happen, well, we'll just take things into our own hands. Ever been there? If so, you certainly have company with Rebekah (both of us Rebekahs!).

---

1 https://www.goodreads.com/quotes/search?utf8=%E2%9C%93&q=god%27s+will+tim+keller&commit=Search, accessed September 12, 2019

We have been studying Sarah's story, and Rebekah was Sarah's daughter-in-law. (The two women never met one another, though, as Sarah passed away shortly before Rebekah married into the family.) After Hagar had Abraham's son Ishmael, Sarah eventually became pregnant herself and gave birth to Isaac, who became husband to Rebekah and father to twins, Jacob and Esau.

Trouble was brewing from the very beginning. (The twins even fought while still in the womb—see Genesis 25:22-23.) Making the family dynamics worse, parents Isaac and Rebekah played favorites; Isaac preferred Esau, and Rebekah's favorite was Jacob. This is seen most clearly in the passage quoted above from Genesis 27. Isaac was on his deathbed and desired to give his son Esau a special blessing. Rebekah, catching wind of the plan, schemed with Jacob (perhaps her influence is to blame for Jacob then being known for quite a while afterwards as the deceiver?) to get Isaac to bestow that special blessing on Jacob instead.

What is particularly sad about this scheme is that it is this very plan of deception that led to a years-long schism between brothers—a schism that often led Esau to want to go so far as to murder Jacob. God later heals the broken relationship in a wonderfully touching reconciliation story that you can read about in Genesis 32, but the damage was nevertheless done for many years to come—all because Rebekah took it upon herself to operate according to her own plan and her own desires and influenced her son to do the same.

Sometimes, in order to break ourselves away from our daily distractions in true Lenten fashion and instead grow our intimacy with God and surrender to His will, we will be required to give up plans, desires, and goals that really mean a lot to our hearts—not just things that we would "kinda like" to see happen but don't really care one way or another if they don't come to pass. No, I'm talking about things that are soul level, heartfelt, and incredibly important to us— things that we want so desperately to happen that, if they don't, we wonder how we will go on.

This is where knowing and relying on sound theology comes in. We will only be able to willingly relinquish our own plans and desires if we trust that God knows best and operates in our lives out of a heart of immense love, care, and concern for us. We will only trust God in this way if we love Him deeply, and we will only be able to love Him deeply if we truly know Him. I bet you can guess what comes next! We will only truly know Him if we know His Word.

Yes, everything always circles back to the importance of knowing and being in the Word, because it is just that crucial to our ability to live our one life well to the glory of God and the advancement of His kingdom. Paul makes this clear in 2 Timothy 3:16-17:

> All Scripture is given by inspiration of God, and is profitable for doctrine, for reproof, for correction, for instruction in righteousness, that the man of God may be complete, thoroughly equipped for every good work.

It is this very Word of God that encourages us with such perspective-changing and hope-filled truths, such as those contained in passages like Jeremiah 29:11-13 and Romans 8:28:

> "For I know the thoughts that I think toward you," says the Lord, "thoughts of peace and not of evil, to give you a future and a hope. Then you will call upon Me and go and pray to Me, and I will listen to you. And you will seek Me and find Me, when you search for Me with all your heart."

> And we know that all things work together for good to those who love God, to those who are the called according to His purpose.

The reality of these truths does not mean that we will be sheltered from ever having to experience hard, trying, heartbreaking times in our lives. After all, when the prophet Jeremiah penned those words of the Lord's, God's people were at that time enduring what would become a seventy year period of Babylonian exile! And the phrase "all things" in Romans 8:28 refers to just that—the good, the bad, and the ugly.

What is ultimately more encouraging, however, is not the idea that we will get all we want and our own plan for a pain-free life will come to fruition, but rather that even as we go through the ups and downs of life, we will have the Lord God Almighty on our side, serving as our help, hope, and defense through it all. That, my friend, is some pretty great news!

Action Step:

Spend some time in prayer, crying out to God about the desires of your heart and asking for a trusting, surrendered spirit. He understands how you feel and yearns to hear from you and help you in this journey. Also consider meditating on and memorizing Psalm 37:3-5:

> Trust in the Lord, and do good; Dwell in the land, and feed on His faithfulness. Delight yourself also in the Lord, and He shall give you the desires of your heart. Commit your way to the Lord, trust also in Him, and He shall bring it to pass.

Remember, however, that this passage is not meant as a bargaining chip or a way to make God bring your plan to fruition. Rather, it is a lesson on the importance of delighting in the Lord and a reminder of just how truly fulfilling it is to do so.

Prayer:

Lord, help me to delight in You. My head knows that You know what is best and only have my best interests in mind, but help my heart to know it. Help me to reject any stone-fisted hold I have over my own plans, goals, and desires and to release them to You, knowing that what You have for me is far better. Thank You for your sovereign love and care over me, Father. Help me to rest in it with joy. In Jesus' name, Amen.

Day 5

Rachel and the Quest for Fairness

Then Jacob said to Laban, "Give me my wife, for my days are fulfilled, that I may go in to her." And Laban gathered together all the men of the place and made a feast. Now it came to pass in the evening, that he took Leah his daughter and brought her to Jacob; and he went in to her. And Laban gave his maid Zilpah to his daughter Leah as a maid. So it came to pass in the morning, that behold, it was Leah. And he said to Laban, "What is this you have done to me? Was it not for Rachel that I served you? Why then have you deceived me?"

—Genesis 29:21-25

We tend to think, "Life should be fair because God is fair." But God is not life. And if I confuse God with the physical reality of life—by expecting constant good health for example—then I set myself up for crashing disappointment.

—Phillip Yancey[1]

"Life isn't fair." Chances are you heard a parent or grandparent say that to you more than once when you whined and said that something they had decided was "unfair." Or, perhaps you are a parent, and you regularly tell your children the very same thing.

---

1 http://christian-quotes.ochristian.com/christian-quotes_ochristian.cgi?query=fair&action=Search&x=0&y=0, accessed September 12, 2019

While we know that life isn't fair, I think sometimes we have the belief that its unfairness stems solely from us living in a fallen world, and it is only the curse that makes life appear to be unfair. Surely God isn't given to anything which appears to be unfair.

But is that biblically accurate? Is God completely fair? Does the Bible teach that?

We know that God is just, but that is not necessarily the same thing as being fair. Is it "fair" when a couple who desperately wants to care for a precious baby of their own can't get pregnant, while a couple who is on drugs and living a hard life gets pregnant easily with a child they don't even want? Is it "fair" when a God-honoring, Great-Commission-living person passes away in their twenties, while a vile murderer or rapist lives until a ripe old age? I would venture to say that none of this appears to be fair, right? And while we are not to rely on our feelings to determine truth and, in this case, whether or not God is fair in all His ways, I do believe there is an important Scriptural point to be made here:

> *The Gospel itself reveals that God does not always do what is "fair." And that is good news for us!*

If God were "fair" as we humans define fairness, we would be doomed. Think about it for a moment. What is "fair" about the Easter celebration coming up in a few weeks? What is "fair" about a holy God choosing to give His Son as a sacrifice for fallen, sinful man? What is "fair" about the words of Isaiah 53? Verse 5 says, "But He *was* wounded for our transgressions, He was bruised for our iniquities; the chastisement for our peace was upon Him, and by His stripes we are healed." There isn't anything "fair" about that! But praise God it isn't fair, right?

What we need to understand, though, is that while it is actually a good thing that God is not completely "fair" all the time in His treatment of us, the unfairness of life itself usually doesn't feel like a good thing. The unfairness of this life doesn't usually give us the feelings of being loved and treasured as does the truth of the gospel. Instead, it commonly makes us feel as if God has fallen asleep at the wheel, and the world is turned upside down. It usually evokes feelings of anger, frustration, and hurt.

Rachel was no stranger to these feelings. As we are going down the family tree which began with Abraham and Sarah, we now come to Rachel, Rebekah's daughter-in-law, who was married to Rebekah's favorite son, Jacob.

Apparently, crazy deception ran in the family. Just as Rebekah and Jacob banded together to deceive Isaac, so, too, Rebekah's brother, Laban, deceived Jacob. Jacob had met and had quickly fallen in love with Rachel, Laban's beautiful daughter. He agreed to work for Laban seven years in exchange for being allowed to marry her. (Patriarchy comes to the forefront again, my friends.)

At the end of the seven years and on what was to be Jacob's wedding night with Rachel, Laban deceived Jacob and gave his daughter Leah to Jacob instead. And so begins another years-long season of family drama in Jacob's life! This guy just can't seem to get away from it!

This deception by their father, Laban, pitted Leah and Rachel against each other and led to their becoming fierce competitors. For a long time, Leah was heartbroken, for Jacob seemed to only love Rachel. Meanwhile, Rachel, too, was heartbroken, for she had to share the man she loved with her sister. Not only that, but Leah was repeatedly getting pregnant and giving birth to sons, while Rachel remained infertile for many years. Even once Rachel began to be able to have children, the joy was not terribly long-lasting, as she ended up dying in childbirth with one of her sons.

Rachel had clearly been treated unfairly by her father and his scheme, and the result was much heartache for everyone involved in this bizarre love triangle. Human-induced unfairness hurts, it does damage, and sometimes it destroys lives forever. This is precisely why we mustn't rely on the idol of fairness to bring us joy, fulfillment, and contentment. We must instead look to Christ.

This Easter, shift your focus from the unfair circumstances of your life right now to the good news of the gospel of Christ. Let go of the feeling of it being unfair that you can't afford a new Easter dress this year while your best friend can, or the feeling that it is unfair all the work you must do to clothe, feed, and prepare your children for church this Easter Sunday. Let go of all that and instead rest in the glorious good news of the gospel for you. Rejoice that, as we saw yesterday, God's plan is undoubtedly better than ours—even when it seems unfair, even when this fallen world seems to be messing everything up. God is still good, He is still faithful, He is still kind, He is still sovereign, and He is still to be trusted. Store that truth down deep in your heart today and every day.

Action Step:

Get out a piece of paper and make a list of all the ways in which the truth and implications of the gospel are not "fair." Then keep that list in a place you can turn to regularly when you are tempted to despair over the unfairness of life. Rejoice in God's goodness to you today.

Prayer:

Lord, I know I so often whine like a toddler to you over how unfair is this life. Thank You for being patient with me, for actually wanting me to come to You when I am feeling this way, and for wanting me to be open and honest with You, pouring out all my thoughts no matter what they are. And thank You that You rescue and heal me from those dark thoughts when I lay them at Your feet. Thank You for the unfairness of the gospel—the very unfairness which leads to my forgiveness and restoration in You. Help me to meditate on it when the going gets tough, and I am angry over the unfairness of life. Thank You for being Who You are. In Jesus' name, Amen.

Day 6

Leah and the Quest for Love

She conceived again and bore a son, and said, "Now this time my husband will become attached to me, because I have borne him three sons." Therefore his name was called Levi....Then Leah conceived again and bore Jacob a sixth son. And Leah said, "God has endowed me with a good endowment; now my husband will dwell with me, because I have borne him six sons." So she called his name Zebulun.

—Genesis 29:34; 30:19-20

Satan is ever seeking to inject that poison into our hearts to distrust God's goodness—especially in connection with his commandments. That is what really lies behind all evil, lusting and disobedience. A discontent with our position and portion, a craving from something which God has wisely held from us. Reject any suggestion that God is unduly severe with you. Resist with the utmost abhorrence anything that causes you to doubt God's love and his lovingkindness toward you. Allow nothing to make you question the Father's love for his child.

—A. W. Pink[1]

Can you imagine what it would be like to be Leah? We touched on her story a bit yesterday when discussing her sister, Rachel, but today we will zero in on her side of things. She was the eldest of Laban's daughters (meaning that, in that type of patriarchal culture,

1 http://christian-quotes.ochristian.com/christian-quotes_ochristian.cgi?query=god%27s+love&action=Search&x=0&y=0, accessed September 13, 2019

she must be married off first as the eldest daughter—see Genesis 29:26) and described in this way: "Leah's eyes were delicate, but Rachel was beautiful of form and appearance" (Genesis 29:17).

There was Leah, stuck in the culture of the time and forced to be married to a man who didn't love her but loved her younger, far more beautiful sister instead. Her story reads like a soap opera, but sadly it was true and precisely what Leah endured. For some time, she also endured a near constant feeling of being unloved and unwanted, first by her father and then by her husband.

In Genesis 29 and 30 we see a desperation on Leah's part. She is desperate for her husband to love her and, because of the cultural teachings of the day, believes that if she can only bear enough sons for her husband, he will finally love her. She tries again and again to earn his love, going through pregnancy and childbirth three, four, five, six times, all out of the hope that "now this time my husband will become attached to me" and "now my husband will dwell with me."

Though bearing children may not be the primary way in which women seek to earn love today, it does still happen. And there are a multitude of other ways in which women strive to earn love. Some change the way they dress, others change the way they look, while still others may change how they eat, live, exercise, rest, work, or speak in order to try to earn the love of others. Much of the selfie culture on social media is truly nothing more than our attempt to earn the love, admiration, respect, praise, and attention of others.

When believers act in this same manner, what it reveals is a lack of understanding the love of God for us, His children. Romans 8:31-39 says,

> What then shall we say to these things? If God is for us, who can be against us? He who did not spare His own Son, but delivered Him up for us all, how shall He not with Him also freely give us all things? Who shall bring a charge against God's elect? It is God who justifies. Who is he who condemns? It is Christ who died, and furthermore is also risen, who is even at the right hand of God, who also makes intercession for us. Who shall separate us from the love of Christ? Shall tribulation, or distress, or persecution, or famine, or nakedness, or peril, or sword? As it is written: "For Your sake we are killed all day long; We are accounted as sheep for the slaughter." Yet in all these things we are more than conquerors through Him who loved us. For I am persuaded that neither death nor life, nor

angels nor principalities nor powers, nor things present nor things to come, nor height nor depth, nor any other created thing, shall be able to separate us from the love of God which is in Christ Jesus our Lord.

Truly, if we want to know whether or not God loves us, all we need to do is keep our eyes fixed on the cross, and we will know all we need to know about the depth and richness of His love.

As we are in the middle of the Lenten season and focusing on cutting away the distractions that seek to woo us away from Christ on a daily basis, something important to note is that sometimes one of the reasons we are so distracted is that we are striving to earn love.

We feel we can't just "be still and know" (see Psalm 46:10), because then we wouldn't be accomplishing anything to earn love or prove our worth. The ironic and sad reality, however, is that this thought process, which is so antithetical to the gospel, is keeping us from being able to know, grasp, and live in light of the gospel of Christ and the love that is already ours.

If you are yearning for love, friend, look no further than the cross of Christ. We will go into this further during the last week of our study time together, but for now, remember this: Jesus willingly chose to go to the cross for you. He was broken, punished, beaten, bruised, betrayed, and killed because He loved you and wanted to make a way for you to spend eternity with Him in Heaven. That is how much you are loved. Your quest to earn His love can be over.

Action Step:

Camp out in Romans 8 for a while and consider even committing it to memory. Get out a Bible concordance or look up online verses pertaining to God's love and spend some time poring over them. That way, the next time you feel as if you are unloved or have to earn love, you will be able to recall to mind the truths of God's Word.

Prayer:

Lord, thank You for Your love! Thank You that I don't have to do anything to prove myself, make myself good enough, or work and earn my way into Your good graces. Thank You that You love me just because You are You, and Your very nature itself is love. Help me to know, believe, and call to mind the great depths of Your love for me the next time I am tempted to doubt. And help me to be a conduit of Your love to others. In Jesus' name, Amen.

Day 1

Dinah and the Quest for an Advocate

Now Dinah the daughter of Leah, whom she had borne to Jacob, went out to see the daughters of the land. And when Shechem the son of Hamor the Hivite, prince of the country, saw her, he took her and lay with her, and violated her.

—Genesis 34:1-2

One of the best concepts to describe what it means to 'put on the Lord Jesus Christ' is to become advocates.

—Dhati Lewis[1]

We have already seen two major incidents of turmoil and heartache in Jacob's life. When we turn the page to Genesis 34, we are confronted with yet another—and it is pretty horrific. That chapter of Genesis begins with the words quoted above. Jacob's daughter, Dinah, went to visit the young women of the area and, while on her journey, was raped by Shechem. As if that were not awful enough, what follows would be unbelievable if we didn't know the Word of God to be thoroughly true!

Genesis 34:5-10 says,

And Jacob heard that he had defiled Dinah his daughter. Now his sons were with his livestock in the field; so Jacob held his peace until they came. Then Hamor the father of Shechem went out to Jacob to speak with him. And the sons of Jacob came in

1 Dhati Lewis, *Advocates: The Narrow Path to Racial Reconciliation* (Nashville, Tennessee: B&H Publishing Group 2019) pg. 37

from the field when they heard *it;* and the men were grieved and very angry, because he had done a disgraceful thing in Israel by lying with Jacob's daughter, a thing which ought not to be done. But Hamor spoke with them, saying, "The soul of my son Shechem longs for your daughter. Please give her to him as a wife. And make marriages with us; give your daughters to us, and take our daughters to yourselves. So you shall dwell with us, and the land shall be before you. Dwell and trade in it, and acquire possessions for yourselves in it."

Verses 11-17 continue,

Then Shechem said to her father and her brothers, "Let me find favor in your eyes, and whatever you say to me I will give. Ask me ever so much dowry and gift, and I will give according to what you say to me; but give me the young woman as a wife." But the sons of Jacob answered Shechem and Hamor his father, and spoke deceitfully, because he had defiled Dinah their sister. And they said to them, We cannot do this thing, to give our sister to one who is uncircumcised, for that would be a reproach to us. But on this condition we will consent to you: If you will become as we *are,* if every male of you is circumcised, then we will give our daughters to you, and we will take your daughters to us; and we will dwell with you, and we will become one people. But if you will not heed us and be circumcised, then we will take our daughter and be gone."

Yet again, we see Jacob's deceptive streak rising to the surface. The rest of Genesis 34 is quite a harrowing tale of Jacob's sons secretly attacking Shechem and his entire city while they were incapacitated following their community-wide circumcision. Verses 26-29 describe it this way:

And they killed Hamor and Shechem his son with the edge of the sword, and took Dinah from Shechem's house, and went out. The sons of Jacob came upon the slain, and plundered the city, because their sister had been defiled. They took their sheep, their oxen, and their donkeys, what was in the city and what *was* in the field, and all their wealth. All their little ones and their wives they took captive; and they plundered even all that was in the houses.

And then we come to verse 30:

> Then Jacob said to Simeon and Levi, "You have troubled me
> by making me obnoxious among the inhabitants of the land,
> among the Canaanites and the Perizzites; and since I am few in
> number, they will gather themselves together against me and
> kill me. I shall be destroyed, my household and I."

Now Genesis 35 makes it abundantly clear that our great God is
incredibly merciful and gracious, because Jacob's fears do not come
true. Instead, verse 5 says the terror of God was upon all the cities
surrounding him so that the men there did not end up pursuing
Jacob's sons after all. But imagine how Dinah must have been feeling
throughout this whole ordeal! Here she was, a victim, now likely
feeling as if these brothers of hers, who are supposed to be her defense
and advocate, are instead making things worse for their entire family.

Unfortunately—and not just in this day and age but down through
history—it can be terribly hard to find a true advocate. A most haunting
example of this is found in the words of Deuteronomy 22:25-27:

> But if a man finds a betrothed young woman in the countryside,
> and the man forces her and lies with her, then only the man who
> lay with her shall die. But you shall do nothing to the young
> woman; *there is* in the young woman no sin deserving of death,
> for just as when a man rises against his neighbor and kills him,
> even so *is* this matter. For he found her in the countryside, and
> the betrothed young woman cried out, but there was no one to
> save her.

Ecclesiastes 4:9-12 largely makes the same point as to the
(sometimes serious) importance of having advocates in your life:

> Two are better than one, because they have a good reward for
> their labor. For if they fall, one will lift up his companion. But
> woe to him who is alone when he falls, for he has no one to
> help him up. Again, if two lie down together, they will keep
> warm; But how can one be warm alone? Though one may
> be overpowered by another, two can withstand him. And a
> threefold cord is not quickly broken.

Sadly, we are living in an increasingly isolationist culture. Though we need advocates in our lives, our modern day lifestyles often aren't conducive to the development of the kind of friendship and community we were designed for and need. But what we need to understand is if God has designed us for and called us to the cultivation of friendships and community, then we can choose to live in light of that and adjust our current priorities accordingly in ways that will fit well in our current season of life. All we need are willing hearts to heed the call and the gumption to follow God's guidance.

The timing for this shifting of priorities could not be better as we are in the Lenten season of clearing out of our lives that which is both distracting us and stuffing our lives to the brim with what is not important from an eternal perspective. In this forty-day journey of stepping back from some of the things which are keeping us from mindfully living in light of the gospel in our day-to-day lives, consider what choices need to be made so that you might prioritize the finding and nurturing of God-given, soul-enriching, life-giving advocates. You will be glad you did!

Action Step:

Pursue community. Seek and initiate friendship. Prioritize and pursue it. It will be well worth the effort! Text a friend you haven't gotten together with in a while or call up a gal you've been meaning to reach out to and get to know. Set a coffee date on the calendar and see what happens!

Prayer:

Lord, I know that my current hustle and bustle lifestyle isn't what You intended or how You created life to function. And yet, I don't always know what to do to change it. I don't feel like I know the best place to start. And sometimes, when I do reach out to others, the invitations are not reciprocated, and I get discouraged. But please help me not to give in to those fears. Help me to remember that You will be with me every step of the way and will send the friends into my life with whom you desire for me to grow. Thank You for the gift of community, Father. Help me to treasure it more. In Jesus' name, Amen.

Day 8

Tamar and the Quest for Responsibility

This is the genealogy of Jesus the Messiah the son of David, the son of Abraham: Abraham was the father of Isaac, Isaac the father of Jacob, Jacob the father of Judah and his brothers, Judah the father of Perez and Zerah, whose mother was Tamar.

—Matthew 1:1-3a

God is ready to assume full responsibility for the life wholly yielded to Him.

—Andrew Murray[1]

Imagine for a moment[2] that you are living in a culture where, without warning, you can be taken from your father's home by a stranger and forced to marry someone you have never even met. Imagine further that your value and worth are not found in any gifts or talents you have been personally given by God, any work that you can do, or anything that you can accomplish either before or after you are married.

Instead, your worth is based on whether or not you have children—particularly male children. You are viewed as only being good for the work of continuing a man's family line, passing his name on from one generation to the next, and securing his family's place in history. You aren't seen, valued, or loved for who you are as a person, but rather for what your body can produce. Oh, and if your body can't produce a

---

1 http://christian-quotes.ochristian.com/christian-quotes_ochristian.cgi?query=responsibility&action=Search&x=0&y=0, accessed September 14, 2019

2 A portion of this section first appeared in Rebekah Hargraves, *Good News for a Woman's Heart: An Advent Devotional Study* (Rebekah Hargraves: 2018)

baby? Then you are good for nothing at all. You will likely be relegated to the side while your husband marries a second or even third wife in an effort to procure that idolized progeny he requires.

I imagine you would agree with me when I say that it would be incredibly challenging to succeed in holding on to any hope in such a situation, let alone a desire to bow to the responsibilities and expectations forced upon you by your surrounding culture. And yet, that is precisely what Tamar, an ancestor of our Savior, did.

There are only five women listed in the genealogy of Christ as found in Matthew 1, and the first one we see named is Tamar. The whole of Tamar's story is contained in just one chapter—Genesis 38—with verse six being the first time the Bible mentions her: "Judah got a wife for Er, his firstborn, and her name was Tamar."

Judah "got a wife" for his son. Enter patriarchy again, one of the cultural mores where it is normative for a father to go out and "get" a wife for his son, regardless of whether the two people know each other, love each other, or even want to marry. But marry they must, for a male heir has to be produced.

Following the announcement that Judah has procured a wife for his son, we read in the very next verse that Er is struck down by the Lord for his wickedness. Tamar is now childless and husbandless and, per the patriarchal norm, is sent back to her father's house.

The rest of the story reads like a tragic drama. According to the cultural norms of the day, Er's brother is required to marry Tamar and at least try to produce a son with her on behalf of Er. Instead of living up to his responsibility, however, he refuses to father a son on behalf of his brother and is consequently struck down dead. Judah now has one remaining son, Shelah, whom Judah promises to Tamar as a husband once he (Shelah) is of age (see verse 11).

As we continue to read, we next find that Judah's own wife dies, and, after he recovers from the worst of his grief, he goes on a journey to a place called Timnah. By now, much time has passed, and Tamar has never been given to Shelah in marriage as promised. Instead, she remains in her father's house, a rapidly aging widow.

When Tamar hears of Judah's travels, she decides to meet him on the road to Timnah, wearing the disguise of a prostitute.

This is the point in the account where many people wrongly begin to judge Tamar. Many wrongly assume she has been working as a prostitute, but she has been in her father's house the entire time. However, out of a sense of duty and responsibility to preserve Judah's family line (now that two of his sons are dead, the remaining one has not married, and he has no grandsons), she disguises herself as a prostitute and positions herself in just such a way that Judah will certainly stumble upon her while on his journey.

Tamar's desire is to provide an heir for Judah. Though horrifying to our Western minds, what Tamar does is actually a very selfless move on her part. To be sure, the judgment does not belong on the head of Tamar, but rather on the head of Judah. We find him traveling on a journey when he stumbles upon one he thinks is simply a prostitute by trade and decides to hire her for sex. It's pretty easy to see who the sinful one is in this story.

In a culture in which Tamar is viewed as worthless unless she furthers her father-in-law's family line, Tamar has hope and sees this as her grand opportunity to hold up what she considers to be her side of the bargain, her life responsibility. Judah, however, just wants to have his physical needs and desires met.

In fact, we see Judah admit this himself later in verse 26 when he says, "She is more righteous than I, since I wouldn't give her to my son Shelah." Verse 26 ends with these words: "And he did not sleep with her again."

Maybe you don't live in a patriarchal society wrongly being told that your worth is found in whether or not you are a mother. However, you may very well be facing something in your life right now during this Lenten season that has left you feeling rather hopeless—perhaps a job loss, unmet desire, unreached goal, unfulfilled dream, loss of a loved one, abandonment, financial stress, or health crisis. Whatever it may be that has left you feeling as if there is no hope to be found for you, look up!

Don't fix your eyes on your problems and your (perhaps many) reasons to be lacking in hope this season. Instead, fix your eyes on Christ, the Author and Finisher of your faith (Hebrews 12:2). He is the One who knows the end from the beginning (Isaiah 46:10) and brings good out of it all (Romans 8:28).

Tamar's story was one of hopelessness, trial, disappointment, loss, broken promises, and betrayal. In the midst of it all, however, God was still at work. A baby was born to Tamar—a baby who would be in the lineage of Christ, the coming Messiah, just as Tamar herself would be.

No matter what you are facing today, remember that today is not the end of your story. God has a purpose and a plan. Just think what He could accomplish through you and the portion of your story in which you currently find yourself. There is always reason to hope when we have Christ!

So, no matter what load of responsibility you feel weighing down upon your shoulders this year, let go and let God. Remember that the weight of the world is not ultimately yours to carry. We have our God-given roles and responsibilities, to be sure, but don't allow the busyness, strain, and stress of thinking the responsibility for everything is on you. Remember that God is sovereign and let go of the weight that has been holding you down. Let it go and replace it with the implications of the gospel for you and the finished work of Christ on your behalf.

Action Step:

Sometimes we can't see the forest for the trees and can't even detect the areas in which we are weighing ourselves down with responsibilities that actually aren't even ours to carry. Reach out to your husband, mom, sister, friend, or counselor and ask them if they can detect areas of your life that you have allowed to unnecessarily weigh you down. After all, realizing there is a problem is the first step to recovery!

Prayer:

Lord, please open my eyes to the areas in my life where I am allowing myself to be burdened by concerns You never intended for me to carry. Give me the strength and dedication to relinquish the hold I have on these areas and to enjoy the freedom You came to provide. Thank You for Your abundant freedom, grace, and help, Lord. In Jesus' name, Amen.

Day 9

Ruth and the Quest for Provision

So she gleaned in the field until evening, and beat out what she had gleaned, and it was about an ephah of barley. Then she took it up and went into the city, and her mother-in-law saw what she had gleaned. So she brought out and gave to her what she had kept back after she had been satisfied.

—Ruth 2:17-18

Taken as a whole, the story of Ruth is one of those signs. It was written to give us encouragement and hope that all the perplexing turns in our lives are going somewhere good. They do not lead off a cliff. In all the setbacks of our lives as believers, God is plotting for our joy.

—John Piper[1]

There is a theme that we find among the women listed in the genealogy of Christ,[2] and it is this: God delights in taking the marginalized, judged, hated, used and abused outcasts and bringing them close, showering them with His love and redemption, changing both their stories and their hearts, and revealing His tender Father-heart toward His daughters by forevermore making them into an example of His amazing grace and strength in redemption.

Such is the case with our much-beloved heroine of the faith, Ruth. While the two women in Christ's genealogy, whose stories we have already studied (Tamar and Rahab), are mostly contained in but one

---

1 https://www.goodreads.com/quotes/tag/ruth, accessed September 14, 2019
2 A portion of this section first appeared in Rebekah Hargraves, *Good News for a Woman's Heart: An Advent Devotional Study* (Rebekah Hargraves: 2018)

short chapter of the Bible each, Ruth's story is a bit different—an entire four-chapter book of the Bible is dedicated to her story.

The book of Ruth begins by telling us that there is a famine in the land of Bethlehem, which caused a couple by the name of Elimelech and Naomi to escape, along with their sons, to the country of Moab. While there, Elimelech dies. His sons, Mahlon and Chilion, marry two Moabite women, Orpah and Ruth. Approximately ten years later, Mahlon and Chilion also die, leaving Naomi, Orpah, and Ruth all as widows on the brink of destitution.

Because of the dire straits, financial and otherwise, placed upon widows in a patriarchal culture, Naomi encourages both of her daughters-in-law to each return to her father's house. After much convincing, Orpah finally does so, while Ruth refuses to leave Naomi's side. We see that, at some point, Ruth had clearly renounced the Moabite gods in order to instead follow the God of Israel. In Ruth 1:16-17 she proclaims to Naomi:

> "Entreat me not to leave you,
> Or to turn back from following after you;
> For wherever you go, I will go;
> And wherever you lodge, I will lodge;
> Your people shall be my people,
> And your God, my God.
> Where you die, I will die,
> And there will I be buried.
> The Lord do so to me, and more also,
> If anything but death parts you and me."

These two widowed women, Naomi and Ruth, return to Bethlehem where they now must find a way to provide for themselves. In a culture wherein it would have been very hard to find work as a woman (not to mention the fact that widows were regularly sexually harassed and mistreated in that day), they face a growing mountain of hardship.

In chapter 2 we find resourceful and hardworking Ruth asking that Naomi allow her to glean in the barley field belonging to Boaz, one of her deceased father-in-law's distant relatives. We read that Boaz not only generously allows her to glean in his field, but also ensures that she has access to as much of the harvest as possible, providing Ruth and Naomi with their much-needed sustenance.

As we continue on through the book (which I encourage you to read on your own when you have the chance, as it is a truly beautiful story), we read of the ancient practice of a kinsman redeemer stepping in to act on the behalf of a deceased man. In that day and age, when a man died and his widow was childless, a near relative could act as the kinsman redeemer by marrying the woman, providing for her, and also seeking to produce with her an heir to continue the deceased husband's family line.

Boaz steps in to do all these things and more, providing Ruth with the financial and familial redemption she likely assumed she would never have. As the end of the book tells us,

> So Boaz took Ruth and she became his wife; and when he went in to her, the Lord gave her conception, and she bore a son. Then the women said to Naomi, "Blessed be the Lord, who has not left you this day without a close relative; and may his name be famous in Israel! And may he be to you a restorer of life and a nourisher of your old age; for your daughter-in-law, who loves you, who is better to you than seven sons, has borne him." Then Naomi took the child and laid him on her bosom, and became a nurse to him. Also the neighbor women gave him a name, saying, "There is a son born to Naomi." And they called his name Obed. He is the father of Jesse, the father of David.
>
> —Ruth 4:13-17

If you're doing the math there, this means that Ruth was King David's great-grandmother and, in turn, the great-great-great (and so on!) grandmother of Christ Himself.

Perhaps you relate to Ruth's story this Lenten season. Perhaps you are in dire financial straits, nearly destitute and wondering how you are going to get by. Perhaps you are slaving every day just to try to put food on the table, and your quest for provision is leaving you overworked, worried, and overwhelmed.

What you need to know is this: The God of Ruth is your God, too. He is the same unchanging God yesterday, today, and forever. He is still in the business of changing lives for the better. He is still in the business of being our Jehovah Jireh, our God Who provides. He is still in the business of working miracles. But above all and most importantly, He is in the business of meeting all our needs in Himself.

Ultimately, we mustn't look to a bigger bank account, a husband, a baby, or anything else to make us happy. All will at one time or another disappoint. Instead, we must look to the Lord, the Maker of heaven and earth (Psalm 146:6). We must look to Him Who is able to fill all our deepest longings, ease every heartbreak and pain, and redeem and restore every debilitating loss and hopelessness we feel as we walk through this life. That, my friends, is what we need to cling to when the going—inevitably at some point—gets tough.

We can look to Him, and we can have hope. Just like Ruth.

Action Step:

Spend some time in prayer today, mindfully and intentionally meditating on the fact that, ultimately, God is your provider. He is your Jehovah-Jireh. He is the One who orchestrates details behind the scenes to provide you with what you need. Commit your needs to Him today and see just what He does.

Little bonus step for you: Read George Mueller's autobiography to really have your faith built up in this area!

Prayer:

Lord, my head knows You are my provider, but my heart often doubts. Many days I go through life thinking that the hope of provision resides on my shoulders alone. Break me free from this debilitating burden and from this wrong thinking, and help me to replace these worries with Your truth. Thank You for being my provider and for promising to care for me just as well as, if not better than, You do the sparrows. Help me to remember this truth each time I see a bird—a constant reminder of Your tender loving care. In Jesus' name, Amen.

Day 10

Rahab and the Quest for Peace

"I know that the Lord has given you [i.e., the Israelite spies] the land, that the terror of you has fallen on us, and that all the inhabitants of the land are fainthearted because of you. For we have heard how the Lord dried up the water of the Red Sea for you when you came out of Egypt, and what you did to the two kings of the Amorites who were on the other side of the Jordan, Sihon and Og, whom you utterly destroyed. And as soon as we heard these things, our hearts melted; neither did there remain any more courage in anyone because of you, for the Lord your God, He is God in heaven above and on earth beneath. Now therefore, I beg you, swear to me by the Lord, since I have shown you kindness, that you also will show kindness to my father's house, and give me a true token."

—Joshua 2:9-12

Jericho's walls fell flat: Rahab's house was on the wall, and yet it stood unmoved; my nature is built into the wall of humanity, and yet when destruction smites the race, I shall be secure. My soul, tie the scarlet thread in the window afresh, and rest in peace.

—Charles Haddon Spurgeon[1]

---

1 https://www.goodreads.com/quotes/search?commit=Search&page=4&q=rahab&utf8=□, accessed September 14, 2019

As we have seen already, throughout the Word we are introduced to a number of women who found themselves in hard, challenging, and seemingly hopeless situations. Women who, though things looked bleak for a time, were loved, redeemed, and blessed by God with a life-changing hope and left with an amazing testimony.

This is certainly true of Rahab,[2] the second woman we find mentioned in the genealogy of Christ.

We are first introduced to Rahab in Joshua 2. When Rahab enters the narrative, two Israelite men have just been sent out to Jericho by Joshua. Their mission was to search out the city, the land the Lord would soon give into the hands of the Israelites. They were not simply to search the city, however. They were to study the city with the purpose of taking control of it.

In the midst of this mission, they "went, and came to the house of a harlot named Rahab, and lodged there" (Joshua 2:1). We don't know if the men knew she was a prostitute or not. We don't know if this was Rahab's chosen profession or if she were involved in prostitution out of a sense of desperation or destitution. We know very little about that aspect of the story. We do know Rahab had a family, including a father, mother, and siblings (verse 13), but that's the extent of the information we have as to Rahab's background.

What we do know is that she was a prostitute living in the city wall of Jericho, a city about to be taken over by the nation of Israel. The very city wall, in fact, which will be broken down just a few short chapters later (see Joshua 6), even though it was considered the most important city in the Jordan valley and known as the strongest fortress in all of Canaan.

Here was Rahab, a Canaanite prostitute female living in a doomed city wall. If that doesn't spell hopelessness, I don't know what does! She laments this hopelessness in the verses from Joshua 2 quoted above. Rahab found herself in a desperate situation (not only was the city doomed to destruction, but the elders of the land would have been all too happy to put her to death for harboring the spies!), yet, as Hebrews 11:30-31 points out, in the midst of it all she had faith:

---

2 A portion of this section first appeared in Rebekah Hargraves, *Good News for a Woman's Heart: An Advent Devotional Study* (Rebekah Hargraves: 2018)

> By faith the walls of Jericho fell down after they were encircled for seven days. By faith the harlot Rahab did not perish with those who did not believe, when she had received the spies with peace.

In spite of the fact that she had seemingly been an unbeliever up until this point (and the fear of death—not necessarily a personal belief in the God of Israel—could well have been her first inspiration for saving the spies), she nevertheless seems to have come to saving faith in God as she experienced His grace in sparing her life and the lives of her family.

Though she knew no hope when this whole ordeal first began, she walked away from it with much hope. It was a hope that did not disappoint, for it was hope in the living God of Israel Himself.

What is particularly beautiful about Rahab's story is the picture it is of the restoration and redemption brought about by the grace of God. Rahab began as a prostitute, but her life story ends with her becoming the mother of Boaz, mother-in-law of Ruth, and great (multiple greats!) grandmother of Christ Himself—her Redeemer then and our Redeemer today.

You now have a decision to make, friend. Will you continue believing the lies about who you are, your worth in the eyes of God, and your impact on this world? Rahab most likely believed the lie that her worth was determined by what she could do for the men who employed her. I imagine she believed herself to be worthless at one time or another, beyond redemption, not worthy of God's forgiveness, and incapable of pleasing the God her people so desperately feared.

While it may be true that our sin renders us unworthy of the love and grace of God, that is not how God views us. He views us as the objects of His love, compassion, and concern. Our God is a tender, merciful, abundantly forgiving God toward anyone who comes to Him in repentance and faith. It doesn't matter what labels you have been wearing, whether a scarlet "A" or something else entirely. It doesn't matter how other people view you or what they have grown to expect from you or what you may think is your worth. What matters is how the God of the universe views you and what He has to say about you.

It matters that Immanuel, God with us, came to earth as a tiny baby to save us from our sins, no matter how great they may be. And it matters that that baby grew up into the God-Man Who died on the cross on our behalf. It doesn't matter how big your sin—God's love is bigger. It doesn't matter how black your sin—God's redeeming grace makes you whiter than snow. It doesn't matter how many lives you have hurt by your example—God's omnipotence is greater, He can still bring good out of the bad, and He can still redeem lives you have sought to destroy. That is the source of our hope, just as it was for Rahab.

If you ever doubt that God is ready, willing, and able to save you to the uttermost, just look at our sister, Rahab—the harlot, the woman, the pagan Canaanite living in a city destined to belong to Israel, the people of God. We would think the Israelites would hate and despise such a woman as Rahab. But that didn't matter, because God loved her. And that's what makes all the difference in the world.

If you are desperately seeking for peace in your life this Lenten season, friend, look no further than the same God to whom Rahab looked. As my friend, Amber, has written, "Peace is the very nature of God.... Peace on Earth comes only through Jesus." And it is peace which our God yearns to give us. Consider these passages as you go throughout your day:

> Peace I leave with you, My peace I give to you; not as the world gives do I give to you. Let not your heart be troubled, neither let it be afraid.
>
> —John 14:27

> Be anxious for nothing, but in everything by prayer and supplication, with thanksgiving, let your requests be made known to God; and the peace of God, which surpasses all understanding, will guard your hearts and minds through Christ Jesus.
>
> —Philippians 4:6-7

Action Step:

Surrender your burdens to the Lord. Let go of the striving for peace and find it in Christ—at this moment and in every moment which lies ahead.

Prayer:

Lord, You know how broken this world is. You know how much I desperately needed this Lenten season of stepping back from the craziness of the world to fix my eyes on You. I feel like I am seriously lacking in peace right about now, but I know that You promise to give me peace when I pour out my burdens to You. In fact, because of the gospel, I have already been given Jesus' peace. Help me to live in light of it today and every day. Thank You for Your amazing grace in abundance, Lord. In Jesus' name, Amen.

Day 11

Bathsheba and the Quest for Justice

It happened in the spring of the year, at the time when kings go out to battle, that David sent Joab and his servants with him, and all Israel; and they destroyed the people of Ammon and besieged Rabbah. But David remained at Jerusalem. Then it happened one evening that David arose from his bed and walked on the roof of the king's house. And from the roof he saw a woman bathing, and the woman was very beautiful to behold. So David sent and inquired about the woman. And someone said, "Is this not Bathsheba, the daughter of Eliam, the wife of Uriah the Hittite?" Then David sent messengers, and took her; and she came to him, and he lay with her.

—2 Samuel 11:1–4a

Ahab cast a covetous eye at Naboth's vineyard, David a lustful eye at Bathsheba. The eye is the pulse of the soul; as physicians judge of the heart by the pulse, so we by the eye; a rolling eye, a roving heart. The good eye keeps minute time, and strikes when it should; the lustful, crochet-time, and so puts all out of tune.

—Thomas Adams[1]

Matthew 1:6b says, "David the king begot Solomon by her who had been the wife of Uriah." Though not expressly named here in Matthew, we know this verse to be referring to Bathsheba, the

---

1 http://christian-quotes.ochristian.com/christian-quotes_ochristian.cgi?query=bathsheba&action=Search&x=0&y=0, accessed September 14, 2019

woman with whom King David had an affair.[2] What is particularly sad about the way in which many Bible teachers handle this account is that oftentimes Bathsheba is the primary one who is blamed for the sin committed by King David. To help illustrate for us why this is an unfair and an unbiblical treatment of the story, all we need to do is take a look at how the relationship between King David and Bathsheba is described at the beginning of 2 Samuel 11.

Several telling statements in this narrative point to David as being the one to blame here, not Bathsheba (even though she is commonly demonized in our day):

First, because it was springtime, it was David's duty as king to go out to battle. He chose instead to remain at home and sent Joab and his servants in his place. This failure to live up to his duty as the ruler of Israel was the first mistake he made, and it was that which put him in the perfect position to fall into temptation.

Second, it's important to note that, interestingly enough, Bathsheba was actually not even bathing in her own home. Nor was she seductively bathing in a public fashion with the intent of causing a man to stumble, as certain Bible commentators attempt to claim. What she was doing was faithfully observing the Old Testament ceremonial law found in Leviticus 15, which said women had to bathe in a particular fashion following the end of their menstrual cycle. (Proof of this is found in 2 Samuel 11:4.)

As Libby Anne points out,[3]

> According to Jewish law, women are made unclean by their menstrual period. After it is over and a certain number of days have passed, they must take a ritual bath in a mikveh. Bathsheba went to the mikveh. She was not simply taking a bath. Furthermore, she would not have chosen the location. The ritual bath requires full immersion, and the mikveh must be built to specific requirements. People didn't have their own mikvehs in their homes—Bathsheba would have gone to the community mikveh. The mikveh isn't like a bathing tub that could be moved; it is more like the Christian baptismal, which are built into churches specifically for baptisms.

---

2 A portion of this section first appeared in Rebekah Hargraves, *Good News for a Woman's Heart: An Advent Devotional Study* (Rebekah Hargraves: 2018)

3 http://www.patheos.com/blogs/lovejoyfeminism/2014/02/ctbhhm-davids-sin-was-all-bathshebas-fault.html?fbclid=IwAR2xGL_ROOqiWeL99LUlemXb4REA-QR0UT-F-UGNMC4xjiNs-fxP8Px-b7B0

Libby continues,

> [Bathsheba] went to the community mikveh and bathed according to the requirements of the law. David was walking the roof of his palace, which would have been one of the highest buildings in Jerusalem, and from that height he saw her bathing in the community mikveh. The mikveh walls were not tall enough to conceal Bathsheba from the eyes of a man on the roof of the palace, but that was not her doing. David sends a servant to find out who she is because she was at the community mikveh, not in her own home—if she'd been bathing at her house and he'd seen her there, he would simply have needed to find out whose house it was. Bathsheba was not tempting David. She was not being "immodest." She was not trying to get his attention. She was following the Jewish law and doing what every other woman did—bathing naked in the community mikveh several days after her period, to purify her ritual uncleanness.

To somehow view the text through modern, Western eyes and thereby come to the conclusion that Bathsheba was seductively bathing for all the world to see is a case of twisting and adding to the text and ignoring the historical context.

Third, the Word says David "took her" (2 Samuel 11:4, 2 Samuel 12:4, 9). This is the language of force. What is incredibly sad about this whole story is that, far from being a seductress or vixen, the real likelihood is that Bathsheba was actually a victim of rape. David inquired after her, sent for her, took her, and lay with her, knowing full well that she was a married woman.

Think for a moment how Bathsheba must have been feeling as this whole sordid story began to play out. Far from the picture some paint of Bathsheba as a flirtatious, loose, Proverbs 7 type woman bent on bringing down King David, she was in all likelihood the victim. Because she was home alone as her husband, Uriah, was out fighting in the army (where David himself was supposed to be), when she discovered that she was being summoned by the king, she probably felt one primary emotion: grief. Why? Because, as a military wife myself, I imagine her first thought upon hearing that the king wanted to meet with her would be the same thought I would have if a dark car containing two men dressed in military uniform pulled up in front of my house: *My husband has died in the war.*

Here she is thinking she is having a meeting with the king, when in reality she is walking into a far more intimate encounter. Not only does King David have what at first appears to be a one night stand with her (this is the best case scenario; the worst case scenario is that he actually raped her), he then proceeds to intentionally have her husband, Uriah, killed in battle. Her worst fear comes true. Her husband is dead now—at the very hands of the king who had his way with her.

The initial encounter between Bathsheba and King David results in Bathsheba conceiving a son who, to make matters even worse, is doomed to die as a result of his father's sin (2 Samuel 12:13-23). Bathsheba's story goes from bad to worse as she grieves the loss of her first husband and now must grieve the loss of her little son.

From then on, Bathsheba all but fades into obscurity. Little else is said of her in the Word, apart from the fact that she goes on to conceive and bear David's son, Solomon, who would become known as the wisest man who ever lived. By and large, Bathsheba's story consists of much loss, heartache, trial, and mistreatment. We don't even have much to prove that King David ever actually truly, deeply, tenderly loved Bathsheba. In fact, David himself was already married when he took Bathsheba to be his wife. (Saul had given his daughter Michal to be David's wife back in 1 Samuel 18, and he had also married Abigail back in 1 Samuel 25.) Bathsheba was certainly lusted after, but whether or not David truly loved her? That we don't know.

How does Bathsheba's heartbreaking story speak to us today when we feel as if justice is hard to be found in our own lives? Well, we are reminded that even if man mistreats us, even if we feel unloved, hurt, and betrayed, we always, always have the Lord to lean on. His love is sure, His compassion and grace unending, and His acceptance and approval eternal when we are covered in the blood of His Son.

Friend, as we are well on our way through our Lenten journey together, I pray that you are beginning to see and understand the depth of Christ's love for you. Just as He included women in His genealogy who were used and abused, mistreated, unloved, misjudged, and even thrown to the side, so, too, He seeks to include you in His family. Answer the call to follow Him with all your heart, soul, mind, and strength. He yearns to be your Heavenly Father and to adopt you forevermore into His eternal kingdom and redeemed family. His love is for you, friend. Let that realization bring you hope today.

I don't know what is your personal story, but this Lent, if you have been striving for justice, seeking vindication, and feeling overwhelmed by a sense of being alone, step back from those lies and replace them with truth. God promises in Romans 12:19, "Beloved, do not avenge yourselves, but rather give place to wrath; for it is written, 'Vengeance is mine, I will repay,' says the Lord." Psalm 37:28 says, "For the Lord loves justice, and does not forsake His saints; they are preserved forever, but the descendants of the wicked shall be cut off." Take this hope with you today, friend, and may it free you from the oppressive distraction of seeking justice for yourself, which has kept you from remembering and meditating on the gospel for you.

Action Step:

Let go. Let go of the pain, the unforgiveness, the vengeance, the desire to procure retribution yourself and on your own terms. Let go and let God be God in your life. He won't let you down.

Prayer:

Lord, help me to forgive the person who has wronged me. Sometimes I think that forgiving them means excusing what they have done, but I know that isn't the case. What they did is still wrong, but having a forgiving heart frees me from the bondage of bitterness and the constant replaying in my head of what has been done to me. Thank You that You are a God of justice, always coming to the defense of Your people. What a peaceful rest that affords me. Help me to remember and walk in light of that truth. In Jesus' name, Amen.

Day 12

Abigail and the Quest for What's Right

Now when Abigail saw David, she dismounted quickly from the donkey, fell on her face before David, and bowed down to the ground. So she fell at his feet and said: "On me, my lord, on me let this iniquity be! And please let your maidservant speak in your ears, and hear the words of your maidservant. Please, let not my lord regard this scoundrel Nabal. For as his name is, so is he: Nabal is his name, and folly is with him! But I, your maidservant, did not see the young men of my lord whom you sent. Now therefore, my lord, as the Lord lives and as your soul lives, since the Lord has held you back from coming to bloodshed and from avenging yourself with your own hand, now then, let your enemies and those who seek harm for my lord be as Nabal. And now this present which your maidservant has brought to my lord, let it be given to the young men who follow my lord."

—1 Samuel 25:23-27

Obey God and leave all the consequences to Him.

—Charles Stanley[1]

O ne of the biggest issues which leads to our sense of overwhelm, distractedness, and stress in our everyday lives is thinking that we have to do what everyone else is doing or meet the expectations placed upon us by others. Moms especially feel the weight of this every single day as we read study after differing study as to what is supposedly "best" for our kids. Add to that the pain some wives feel who are in marriages with unbelieving husbands who expect them

---

1 https://www.goodreads.com/quotes/tag/obey-god, accessed September 16, 2019

to do things which are contrary to what God's Word says. It can be so hard to know how to navigate the murky waters of life when we are being faced by demands, expectations, and requests on every side, many of which may in some way contradict God's own desires for us.

Interestingly, in 1 Samuel 25, Abigail directly goes against her husband Nabal's sinful wishes and actually brings about much good from having done so.[2] We read in verse 11 that Nabal absolutely did not want David to be fed from his provisions, saying, "Shall I then take my bread and my water and my meat that I have killed for my shearers, and give it to men when I do not know where they are from?" And yet in verses 18-19 we read,

> Then Abigail made haste and took two hundred loaves of bread, two skins of wine, five sheep already dressed, five seahs of roasted grain, one hundred clusters of raisins, and two hundred cakes of figs, and loaded them on donkeys. And she said to her servants, "Go on before me; see, I am coming after you." But she did not tell her husband Nabal.

Abigail knew her husband didn't want David and his men to be fed from his own provisions, and yet she did that very thing anyway. Verses 32-34 then show us that it was actually the Lord Who led her to do this:

> Then David said to Abigail: "Blessed is the Lord God of Israel, who sent you this day to meet me! And blessed is your advice and blessed are you, because you have kept me this day from coming to bloodshed and from avenging myself with my own hand. For indeed, as the Lord God of Israel lives, who has kept me back from hurting you, unless you had hurried and come to meet me, surely by morning light no males would have been left to Nabal!" So David received from her hand what she had brought him, and said to her, "Go up in peace to your house. See, I have heeded your voice and respected your person."

There is no sign whatsoever that God was displeased with Abigail for going against her husband's sinful wishes. Rather, we see that it was God's will for her to do so, and He blessed her obedience to Him.

---

2 This devotional is based on a blog post I wrote, entitled "What Should I do if My Husband Asks Me to Sin?" - https://www.hargraveshomeandhearth.com/what-should-i-do-if-my-husband-asks-me-to-sin/

Similarly, Ezekiel 18 is an entire chapter dedicated to this topic of personal responsibility for doing what is right, and in verses 19-20 we read,

> But you ask, "Why isn't the son punished for his father's sin?" It is because the son has done what is fair and right. He obeyed my rules and followed them. He will certainly live. The person who sins will die. A son will not be punished for his father's sins, and a father will not be punished for his son's sins. The righteousness of the righteous person will be his own, and the wickedness of the wicked person will be his own.

Likewise, in the New Testament we read in Galatians 6:4-5, "But let each one test his own work, and then his reason to boast will be in himself alone and not in his neighbor. For each will have to bear his own load." Romans 14:10, 12 says, "For we will all stand before the judgment seat of God. So then each of us will give an account of himself to God."

The bottom line is this: We will each give a personal account of both our own sin and our own rightdoing to God. Our account will not be based on what our husband said or did or "made" us do, but on what we said and did and chose to do. We will not get brownie points from God for following after the expectations of our husbands—or others—if we know for a fact that they go against our conscience before God. No, if we choose to submit ourselves to a sinful command or something that is less than God's best for our family, that is on us, just as it was on Adam for willfully choosing to sin in the garden. Our responsibility will not be cleared because we were simply submitting to our husband or blindly following what a friend said we should do. We will be responsible when we willingly go along with what we knew was not best for our families.

Though this may seem scary and even more stress-inducing than just following what others think we should do, it's actually really good news and quite freeing. We see in Acts 5:29 that "we ought to obey God rather than men." This means, then, that we are free to simply walk by the Spirit and heed and follow the guidance and direction of God. This means that we don't have to attempt to sort through all the varying voices out there or work ourselves to the bone trying to please everyone and fulfill all their expectations. We are free to instead just follow One—the Lord God Himself Whose design and plan for us is far better than anyone else's ever could be.

This Lent, let the expectations and commands of others go. (This of course doesn't mean that you should not submit to your husband in areas not involving sin, or that you should turn a deaf ear to the true wisdom and good counsel of trusted advisers in your life—that should go without saying!) Ignore Pinterest if it serves to be your downfall with its Easter decoration tutorials, ideas for the "perfect" family Easter outfit ensemble, or menu for the "best" Easter dinner. Instead, relieve yourself of much of the overwhelm, distraction, and information and opinion overload this season by instead inclining your ear to God's voice. It is the only one that will never lead you astray and never be a burden to you.

Action Step:

Make a list of the things that you know, without a doubt, God has called you to in this season: work responsibilities, ministry endeavors, family commitments, etc. Now write down how you believe God has called your own unique family to operate: what your family culture looks like, how your family mission statement is worded, what are your likes, dislikes, and priorities. Now stick to those. This isn't to say that things can't or won't change over time. But at least go with what you know God has led you to for right now and stick to it, turning a deaf ear to any outside voice that is not lining up with the voice of the Holy Spirit in your life.

Prayer:

Lord, thank You for the freedom that I have in You. Thank You that I don't have to bow the knee to every voice, expectation, or opinion of others. Thank You that I can be freed from the rat race to compare when I remain in step with You. Your yoke really is easy, and Your burden really is light. Thank you for that gift. Help me to walk in light of it, daily mindful of the freedom I have in You. In Jesus' name, Amen.

Day 13

Huldah and the Quest for Validation

"Go, inquire of the Lord for me, and for those who are left in Israel and Judah, concerning the words of the book that is found; for great is the wrath of the Lord that is poured out on us, because our fathers have not kept the word of the Lord, to do according to all that is written in this book." So Hilkiah and those the king had appointed went to Huldah the prophetess, the wife of Shallum the son of Tokhath, the son of Hasrah, keeper of the wardrobe. (She dwelt in Jerusalem in the Second Quarter.) And they spoke to her to that effect. Then she answered them, "Thus says the Lord God of Israel."

—2 Chronicles 34:21-23a

Huldah's story is notable in the biblical tradition in that her prophetic words of judgement are centered on a written document: she authorizes what will become the core of Scripture for Judaism and Christianity. Her validation of the text thus stands as the first recognizable act in the long process of canon formation. Huldah authenticates a document as being God's word, thereby affording it the sanctity required for a text as authoritative, or canonical.

—Claudia Camp[1]

---

1 https://margmowczko.com/huldah-prophetess/, accessed September 16, 2019

For centuries, the pagan myths and stereotypes of patriarchy[2] have seeped into the church, blurring our understanding of biblical womanhood and misconstruing whole passages of Scripture. For years, women have been made to believe that for them to teach men theology is for them to be in intentional and direct contradiction to God, His design, and His Word.

But this is simply not true. Throughout the Bible, we see instances of women being used by God to spread His truth—to men and women alike. One such example of this—a truly fascinating one at that!—is that of Huldah the prophetess.

You can read her story in its entirety in both 2 Kings 22 and 2 Chronicles 34. Suffice it to say here, however, that she was powerfully used by God to teach correct theology to the men who came to her for guidance, instruction, and wisdom.

We read in both of the chapters referenced above that Hilkiah the High Priest had found the long-since-lost Book of the Law (which scholars believe to have actually been the book of Deuteronomy). Shaphan, his scribe, proceeded to read it aloud before King Josiah. The king, however, was having trouble interpreting it, so he asked his men (a group of five of the most noteworthy men including Hilkiah, the High Priest; Ahikam, the father of the future governor; Achbor, the son of a prophet; Shaphan, the secretary of state; and Asaiah, the king's officer[3]) to go "inquire of the Lord" for him and for all of Judah, so that they might better understand the words contained in the book, as well as ascertain God's future plans for Judah.

Hilkiah and his men did so, intentionally choosing to see Huldah the prophetess (even though the well-known prophet Jeremiah was also prophesying at this same exact point in history). This woman, Huldah, not only faithfully taught the men what was contained in the Book of the Law, but she even went so far as to prophesy about the future and what God would do to the people of Judah. God used this woman and spoke through her to the men. Interesting, isn't it?

Many Christian women today are on the search for validation. They have been sold a bill of goods when it comes to the Bible's supposed patriarchal nature and teachings, when in reality, God's design is something far more freeing and more beautiful than many realize.

<hr>

2 For an in-depth history as to the pagan roots of patriarchy, check out my two-part podcast episode with Rachel Green Miller - https://www.hargraveshomeandhearth.com/074-beyond-authority-and-submission-part-1-with-rachel-green-miller/

3 https://margmowczko.com/huldah-prophetess/, accessed September 16, 2019

Many women are searching for their place in the church, wondering how they can and should serve the Lord, and are being bombarded on a daily basis by differing voices of all kinds.

Regardless of where one lands on the topic of whether or not women should, for example, be senior pastors of churches, the Bible is abundantly clear on at least this: Women and men were both created to be partners in this life, to be Great Commission workers and ambassadors of Christ, to be image bearers of God, and to be faithful proclaimers of God's truth wherever and whenever God leads them to just such an opportunity.

The fact of the matter is that Peter's admonition for us to be always ready "to give a defense to everyone who asks you a reason for the hope that is in you" (see 1 Peter 3:15) is a command given to both men and women. And God uses both men and women every single day to free others through the truths of God's Word and sound theology.

This Lenten season, as you are tempted to search for, strive for, and maybe even fight for validation from anyone and everyone, stop. Let go. Instead, pore over the truths of God's Word. Search out the narratives, the amazing stories God presents to us in His Word that show us how He uses both His sons and His daughters to further His kingdom and set captives free in countless ways.

That is all the validation you need, my friend. Just as God used Huldah, He is ready and willing to use you. Be a student of His Word, be a Berean (see Acts 17:11), and be ready to help others learn to interpret His Word, even as did Huldah, King Josiah, and the men in his court. You don't need to search for, strive for, or work toward validation from others. You already have it from your God.

Action Step:

Read *Vindicating the Vixens: Revisiting Sexualized, Vilified, and Marginalized Women of the Bible*, edited by Sandra Glahn. This book was instrumental in my coming to the understanding of God's view of and design for women as truly outlined in the Word. One of the chapters in the book specifically goes deep in addressing the topic of the role Huldah played as an Old Testament prophetess. It is a most encouraging read!

Prayer:

Lord, thank You for showing me today that being a woman is not a hindrance, something to apologize for, or something "less than." Thank You for Your design for me as a woman and how rich, fulfilling, and truly kingdom-impacting it can be. Help me to be faithful and make a difference by Your power and strength. In Jesus' name, Amen.

Day 14

Deborah and the Quest for Victory and Strength

Now Deborah, a prophetess, the wife of Lapidoth, was judging Israel at that time. And she would sit under the palm tree of Deborah between Ramah and Bethel in the mountains of Ephraim. And the children of Israel came up to her for judgment. Then she sent and called for Barak the son of Abinoam from Kedesh in Naphtali, and said to him, "Has not the Lord God of Israel commanded, 'Go and deploy troops at Mount Tabor; take with you ten thousand men of the sons of Naphtali and of the sons of Zebulun; and against you I will deploy Sisera, the commander of Jabin's army, with his chariots and his multitude at the River Kishon; and I will deliver him into your hand?'" And Barak said to her, "If you will go with me, then I will go; but if you will not go with me, I will not go!" So she said, "I will surely go with you."

—Judges 4:4–9a

Barak had faith, but with hesitancy. In response to God's command, he said, "I'll obey if..." Yet, Deborah didn't abandon Barak for his lack of faith. Rather, she accompanied him and gave him strength in accomplishing God's purpose. We have here a great example of a man and woman partnering as they obey the commands of God.

—Sandra Glahn[1]

---

1 https://bible.org/article/deborah-woman-god-uses, accessed September 16, 2019

Growing up in very conservative Christian circles, it was common for me to hear (or read in books, which was more often the case) that Deborah's leadership in the book of Judges was a blight on Israel's history. I heard many people say in a prominent Christian ministry at the time that for a country to be under the leadership of a woman was for that country to be under a curse from God. (They got this from a faulty interpretation of Isaiah 3:12, if you're curious.) Supposedly, the only reason God would ever raise up a woman to lead or allow a woman to be put in such a position in the civil sphere would be as a last-ditch effort when there were no good men around, or else as a slap in the face wake-up call to the men who were instead supposed to be leading.

And then I read the Bible for myself.[2]

Deborah's story had been one I ignored with all my might during that season of my life years ago. I simply could not reconcile the seemingly beautiful story of Deborah with my belief that female leadership was a curse. So, I did what we all do when a portion of the Bible simply will not fit into our little box of man-made doctrine: I ignored it. I didn't read it. I glossed right over it because it was too much to handle.

I'm not willing to do that anymore, and, praise God, I haven't for almost three years now. When I was finally willing to let go of my preconceived ideas regarding female leadership in the civil sphere and began to allow the Bible to speak for itself without the aid of my faulty hermeneutics, I discovered an absolutely beautiful picture in Judges 4-5. In the midst of a dark and depressing time in Israel's history when the Israelites were under harsh oppression as a result of their sin, God raised up a woman to lead and rescue His people. And not only that, but He also brought a man onto the scene to partner with Deborah and beautifully illustrate for us the design God has always had in mind for men and women: one of mutual support, partnership, and working together (Genesis 1:26-28) to advance the Kingdom of God as fellow aids and encouragers—not as sex objects, seducers, traps, abusers, dominators, or genders that are just so drastically different that they can't even relate to one another anymore.

We see throughout Judges 4 and 5 that Deborah was a woman who feared God and glorified Him with her life. She was His prophet and the judge of His people, and He raised her up to be so.

---

2 A portion of this section is based on an article I wrote - https://www.hargraveshomeand-hearth.com/was-deborahs-leadership-a-blight-on-israels-history/

Some who do not like the idea of a female leader jump in to quickly say that God just raised Deborah up because there were no good men around to get the job done. This is a sad attempt at discrediting the leadership of Deborah for at least two reasons: First of all, the text never says there was a shortage of godly men. Second, Barak was right there and apparently was a good enough man with a strong enough faith to be included by God in the great "Hall of Faith" found in Hebrews 11. No, it isn't that there was a lack of good men. It was that God wanted a woman to lead this time—and that wreaks havoc on the common narrative that female rulers are a curse from God!

It amazes me that I ever thought I could make a case for the myth that Deborah's leadership was a curse on the nation of Israel when a simple, even cursory, reading of the passage clearly proves otherwise. Consider what had been going on when God raises up Deborah as prophetess and judge:

> When Ehud was dead, the children of Israel again did evil in the sight of the Lord. So the Lord sold them into the hand of Jabin king of Canaan, who reigned in Hazor. The commander of his army was Sisera, who dwelt in Harosheth Hagoyim. And the children of Israel cried out to the Lord; for Jabin had nine hundred chariots of iron, and for twenty years he had harshly oppressed the children of Israel.
>
> —Judges 4:1-3

Consider the resulting outcome of Deborah's leadership:

> And then, as Barak pursued Sisera, Jael came out to meet him, and said to him, "Come, I will show you the man whom you seek." And when he went into her tent, there lay Sisera, dead with the peg in his temple. So on that day God subdued Jabin king of Canaan in the presence of the children of Israel. And the hand of the children of Israel grew stronger and stronger against Jabin king of Canaan, until they had destroyed Jabin king of Canaan.
>
> —Judges 4:22-24

I'm pretty sure that sounds like a great blessing, not a curse. And I'm pretty sure the Israelites at that time would have wholeheartedly agreed. In fact, the passage regarding Deborah's term as a judge ends with these words:

> "Thus let all Your enemies perish, O Lord! but let those who love Him be like the sun when it comes out in full strength." So the land had rest for forty years.

> —Judges 5:31

The land had rest for forty years. That sure sounds like a great blessing to me! Imagine the relief the Israelites must have felt after having been under the harsh oppression of King Jabin for twenty years! No, the people of Israel didn't view Deborah and her leadership as a curse or a blight on their nation's history. Far from it! They viewed her as a great blessing from God. And so should we.

Deborah understood something that many of us women struggle with grasping, and that is this: Victory and strength are ours—but in Christ alone. We as women tend to swing to one of two opposite extremes. We either think victory and strength aren't options for us, or else we think that they are, but they are dependent upon us being "enough" and pulling ourselves up by our bootstraps. But neither is true.

What is true is that we are more than conquerors through Christ (see Romans 8:37), victory is most assuredly ours in Christ (see Revelation 21:4 and John 19:30), and our strength is only ever found in and through Him (Philippians 4:13 and 2 Corinthians 12:9-10). That wasn't just true for Deborah; it's true for you, too!

Action Step:

Whatever battle you may be currently facing this Lenten season, meditate on and memorize passages such as Romans 8:37 and Philippians 4:13 to combat any despair or sense of overwhelm you may be currently feeling.

Prayer:

Lord, thank You that victory and strength are mine every moment of every day if I would only remember to tap into Your Holy Spirit and His work in my heart and life. You gave the Spirit as a gift to inspire, convict, teach, guide, help, encourage, and direct me. Help me to remember that and take advantage of this great gift. In Jesus' name, Amen.

Day 15

Gomer and the Quest for Love

When the Lord began to speak by Hosea, the Lord said to Hosea: "Go, take yourself a wife of harlotry and children of harlotry, for the land has committed great harlotry by departing from the Lord." So he went and took Gomer the daughter of Diblaim, and she conceived and bore him a son.

—Hosea 1:2-3

Love without truth is sentimentality; it supports and affirms us but keeps us in denial about our flaws. Truth without love is harshness; it gives us information but in such a way that we cannot really hear it. God's saving love in Christ, however, is marked by both radical truthfulness about who we are and yet also radical, unconditional commitment to us. The merciful commitment strengthens us to see the truth about ourselves and repent. The conviction and repentance moves us to cling to and rest in God's mercy and grace.

—Tim Keller[1]

For years, I was caught up in the bonds of legalism; I was a good little Pharisee, to be sure. I followed all the man-made rules, spouted off what I thought was biblical truth but was really just cultural expectations and traditions, and judged anyone else who did not. All the while, though I didn't fully realize it at the time, I had a terribly faulty and downright sad view of God. I believed Him to be a rigid taskmaster, someone with His proverbial arms crossed across His

1 https://www.goodreads.com/quotes/search?utf8=□&q=unconditional+love+god&commit=
Search, accessed September 16, 2019

chest and scowl on His face anytime I slipped up and did something I shouldn't have. I thought He was displeased with and disappointed in me.

The glorious good news of the gospel is that this is simply never true if we are in Christ. Paul reminds us in Romans 8:1 that despite all the sin issues he still has in his life, which he shares about in Romans 7, there is nevertheless "no condemnation to those who are in Christ Jesus." God's love for His children is unconditional. This is not to say that He does not still discipline His children when needed, or that He isn't saddened when we sin. He absolutely is, for sin always has its consequences, and it saddens His fatherly heart to see His kids go through those consequences. But He is not angry with us or disappointed. After all, He knows we are going to still struggle with sin and slip up and fall! David reminds us of that in the beautiful Psalm that is Psalm 103:

> For as the heavens are high above the earth, so great is His mercy toward those who fear Him; As far as the east is from the west, so far has He removed our transgressions from us. As a father pities his children, so the Lord pities those who fear Him. For He knows our frame; He remembers that we are dust (verses 11-14).

What is so beautiful about this Psalm is that God's awareness of the strong pull that we sometimes feel toward sin and temptation does not cause Him to be angry with us. In fact, it rather causes Him to pity us and to be with us every step of the way, all the while loving and helping us in our struggles. Why? Because His love for us is truly unconditional.

This is what the amazing story of Hosea and Gomer illustrates for us in a rather powerful way. Hosea was a prophet of God, an upright and God-fearing man. Such a man in our day (as no doubt was the case in his) would be expected to search for a wife among the God-fearing women at his local church, the missionaries he knows, or those serving at the local Christian soup kitchen ministry, right? Certainly he would be looking for a God-honoring woman to serve the Lord and partner with in kingdom work throughout the rest of their lives. Surely that is what God Himself would expect, right?

Well, let's just say that was definitely not the case for Hosea. God's plan for him was that he would marry a prostitute. Not only that, but it wasn't as if this prostitute would even leave her profession following their marriage. No, this prostitute returned again and again and again to her prostitution, rejecting and forsaking Hosea's love all along the way. Imagine how heartbreaking that must have been for him!

Now imagine that you are Gomer, and God is Hosea. You see, it was precisely that very reason right there why God called Hosea to marry Gomer in the first place—so that we would know and understand fully the great and insurmountable height of God's love for us. We sin every day. On a daily basis we return again and again and again to many of the same old sins with which we have repeatedly struggled in the past. In so doing, we reject in that moment the love and grace and ways of God and exchange them for the ways of the world. But God still loves us. He still comes after us. He still pursues us. And He still always, always wants us.

That is what makes Hosea and Gomer's story so beautiful and so powerful—it reveals to us the most amazing love that is ours in the Lord. You see, friend, you never have to search for love again. You never have to try to find it, try to keep it, try to earn it, or try to deserve it. All you have to do is embrace and accept it and live in light of it.

This Lenten season, stop your striving. Cease your quest for love and realize that you already possess a far more perfect love than you could ever hope to find in this world. A love that is yours for the taking in Christ. A love that will never ever let you go.

Action Step:

Write out Psalm 103:11-14 on a notecard and take it with you in your purse, post it on a wall of your home, or affix it to a bathroom mirror. Meditate on and believe its truths whenever you see it.

Prayer:

Father, I cannot begin to imagine how You could love me like You do. I cannot imagine why You love me like You do. But I know You do. I believe it, and I embrace it. Help me to rest in it, live in light of it, and spread it to others. Thank You for the gift and the treasure of Your unconditional love for me. In Jesus' name, Amen.

Day 16

Michal and the Quest for an Unsoiled Reputation

So David and all the house of Israel brought up the ark of the Lord with shouting and with the sound of the trumpet. Now as the ark of the Lord came into the City of David, Michal, Saul's daughter, looked through a window and saw King David leaping and whirling before the Lord; and she despised him in her heart. So they brought the ark of the Lord, and set it in its place in the midst of the tabernacle that David had erected for it. Then David offered burnt offerings and peace offerings before the Lord. And when David had finished offering burnt offerings and peace offerings, he blessed the people in the name of the Lord of hosts. Then he distributed among all the people, among the whole multitude of Israel, both the women and the men, to everyone a loaf of bread, a piece of meat, and a cake of raisins. So all the people departed, everyone to his house. Then David returned to bless his household. And Michal the daughter of Saul came out to meet David, and said, "How glorious was the king of Israel today, uncovering himself today in the eyes of the maids of his servants, as one of the base fellows shamelessly uncovers himself!" So David said to Michal, "It was before the Lord, who chose me instead of your father and all his house, to appoint me ruler over the people of the Lord, over Israel. Therefore I will play music before the Lord. And I will be even more undignified than this, and will be humble in my own sight. But as for the maidservants of whom you have spoken, by them I will be held in honor." Therefore Michal the daughter of Saul had no children to the day of her death.

—2 Samuel 6:15-23

If we would be angry and not sin (says one), we must be angry at nothing but sin; and we should be more jealous for the glory of God than for any interest or reputation of our own.

—Matthew Henry[1]

There's no doubt in my mind that David was quite a case. Sure, he was deemed to be a man after God's own heart, but that didn't mean he didn't have issues—because he definitely did! He was married to multiple women and housed many concubines besides, he had what appears to have been a rather forceful affair with Bathsheba, he essentially murdered Bathsheba's husband, and then we read of these issues between him and his wife Michal in 2 Samuel 6.

Now, whether it was Michal or David who was on the right side of this argument, this account nevertheless raises some important issues to consider. After all, isn't a "a good name to be chosen rather than great riches" (Proverbs 22:1a)? Shouldn't we care about what our actions and lifestyle choices are saying about the God Whom we claim to serve?

In a way, yes. We should certainly seek to live upright lives to the praise and glory of God's name. We should do what is right and forsake doing what is wrong. By living in this way, we will naturally develop a reputation for being joyful, peaceful, patient, and so on if we are walking by the Spirit (see Galatians 5:16-23).

But there is a key component here which we often easily forget: The world will always view Christ and His ways as weird, old-fashioned, out of style, or wrong. God's ways are not the ways of the world, nor the ways of our natural, inborn sin nature. This means, then, that sometimes living in accordance with God's standards will mean appearing rather backward to the world. And sometimes it will lead to a soiled reputation in the eyes of the world. The question is, are we okay with that?

Whether it was appropriate for David to dance around nearly naked in the presence of others, and whether that was something God wanted him to do or just something he thought he should do, are certainly questions up for debate. But there was something Michal needed to remember, as well, and that is this: Sometimes the watching

---

1 http://christian-quotes.ochristian.com/christian-quotes_ochristian.cgi?query=reputation&action=Search&x=0&y=0, accessed September 19, 2019

world is going to think we're crazy. And that is okay, as long as we are living lives that bring honor and glory to the Lord.

This Lenten season, where is your focus? Are you striving to appear perfect, normal, and "relevant" to the watching world? Are you trying to impress the world, show them you're hip, and make them think that being a Christian means you can still be pretty much like the world? Or are you willing to appear a little weird for the sake of walking in the footsteps of Christ?

Because the truth of the matter is this: Jesus certainly had a soiled reputation in the eyes of certain folks of His day. Some thought His theology was off, others thought He was a lunatic, still others thought He was loose with His morals because He dined with tax collectors and sinners. But did any of that truly matter? No, because He was walking in step with His Father's ways moment by moment, day by day. He was fulfilling His mission on earth, and that is what was important—regardless of what exactly the watching world had to say about it.

So, friend, consider this your permission to relax, rest, and take a deep breath. Permission to let go of the expectations of others. Permission to delight in whom God made you to be and how He desires for you to live. Permission to live to please an audience of only one—the Lord Himself. The moment we can let all other concerns, fears, people-pleasing tendencies, etc. go is when we will experience the sweet freedom which comes from being concerned only with what the Lord thinks of us. I encourage you to lean into that permission and freedom today. It will be good for your soul!

Action Step:

Make a list of the cultural expectations you are feeling right now—things that other people want you to do, worldly standards you feel as if you have to live up to, etc. Now make a list in a second column, writing out some corresponding truths about what the Lord wants for you instead. For example, in the first list you might have something written down like "I have to be perfect," while in the same line in your second list you might have, "I am being perfected in Christ and already have His righteousness as my own." Whenever you need to, look back on this list and meditate on its truths. Also add to it when the need arises.

Prayer:

Lord, thank You that I don't have to strive to have a "perfect" reputation, whatever that even is. Certainly, I want to live a life that is honoring and glorifying to You, but I know I do not have to strive to live up to the expectations of others. I don't have to always seek an unsoiled reputation. All I have to do is seek to walk by the Spirit and let the proverbial chips fall where they may. Thank You for the encouragement, rest, and peace that are to be found in that truth, and help me to walk in light of it today. In Jesus' name, Amen.

Day 17

Naomi and the Quest for Relief from Pain and Loss

But she said to them, "Do not call me Naomi; call me Mara, for the Almighty has dealt very bitterly with me." So Boaz took Ruth and she became his wife; and when he went in to her, the Lord gave her conception, and she bore a son. Then the women said to Naomi, "Blessed be the Lord, who has not left you this day without a close relative; and may his name be famous in Israel! And may he be to you a restorer of life and a nourisher of your old age; for your daughter-in-law, who loves you, who is better to you than seven sons, has borne him." Then Naomi took the child and laid him on her bosom, and became a nurse to him. Also the neighbor women gave him a name, saying, "There is a son born to Naomi." And they called his name Obed. He is the father of Jesse, the father of David.

—Ruth 1:20; 4:13-17

On every page of the Bible there is recognition that faith encounters troubles. We are broken ourselves and can't escape the brokenness and loss of our fallen world...An honest reading [of Job and Naomi's stories] reveals a God who doesn't explain himself. He didn't tell Job about his earlier conversation with Satan and he didn't give Naomi three good reasons why her world fell apart. Both sufferers went to their graves with their whys unanswered and the ache of their losses still intact. But somehow, because they met God in their pain, both also gained a deeper kind of trust in him that weathers adversity and refuses to let go of God. Their stories coax us to get down to the business of wrestling with God instead of chasing rainbows and to employ the same kind of brutal honesty that they did, if we dare.

—Carolyn Custis James[1]

1 https://www.goodreads.com/quotes/search?utf8=□&q=naomi+ruth&commit=Search, accessed September 19, 2019

Naomi's story is one of so much unimaginable loss and pain, and yet it is also one of so much unimaginable redemption, joy, and legacy. Ruth 1 tells us that Naomi first lost her husband and then, as if that weren't hard enough, lost her two sons as well. She was now a childless widow in a time and culture in which being so was a disgrace and destined a woman to a life of destitution. And yet, all things are possible with God!

Naomi's story begins to change from one of overwhelming grief and sadness to one of impending joy and gladness in Ruth 2. This widow and her widowed daughter-in-law, Ruth, meet a distant relative of theirs, Boaz, who promises to go above and beyond the call of duty to protect and make a way for these ladies to provide for themselves. He saw to it that their needs were met, while also at the same time preserving their dignity in allowing them to work his field so that they could provide for their own needs, rather than simply receive a handout.

One thing leads to another and, before we know it, by the end of the book of Ruth, chapter 4 tells us that Boaz and Ruth end up getting married and having a sweet son of their own, whom they name Obed. As if that weren't amazing enough, this little Obed became the father of Jesse and the grandfather of King David, as well as an ancestor of Jesus Himself. Talk about a story of redemption!

Friend, I don't know what kind of pain you are currently experiencing or what loss you have been through, but I do know this: Our God is a God of redemption! The same God Who wrought miracles in the life of Naomi and her loved ones is the same God Whom you follow today. His heart for Naomi is the same as His heart for you, and He is always working behind the scenes to bring good out of even those seemingly worthless and heart-wrenching moments of our lives.

So, this Lenten season, look to Him, friend. Pour out all your cares, your burdens, your pains, and your heartbreaking losses at His feet. He wants you to do that! First Peter 5:6-7 says, "Therefore humble yourselves under the mighty hand of God, that He may exalt you in due time, casting all your care upon Him, for He cares for you." Turn to Him, friend. He is ready and willing to carry you, help you, and deliver you through this trial safely to the other side.

Action Step:

Take some time to read through all of Naomi's story as contained in the book of Ruth. This may sound like quite a bit of reading, but it is only four chapters long, and you can get through it pretty quickly. Immerse yourself in this true story of God's great power of redemption and watch your faith be built up as you do so. Be sure to have a journal nearby so that you can jot down any thoughts that come to you as you read.

Prayer:

Lord, thank You that You are the same yesterday, today, and forever, and that I don't have to look at stories like that of Naomi and wish that You would work in my heart and life as You did in hers. Instead, I can have faith knowing that You are still in the business of redemption, and You are still bringing good out of not-so-good events in our lives. Help me to hold fast to You and trust in Your good plan. Thank You for Your heart of love, care, and concern for me. In Jesus' name, Amen.

Day 18

Esther and the Quest for a Future

And Mordecai told them to answer Esther: "Do not think in your heart that you will escape in the king's palace any more than all the other Jews. For if you remain completely silent at this time, relief and deliverance will arise for the Jews from another place, but you and your father's house will perish. Yet who knows whether you have come to the kingdom for such a time as this?" Then Esther told them to reply to Mordecai: "Go, gather all the Jews who are present in Shushan, and fast for me; neither eat nor drink for three days, night or day. My maids and I will fast likewise. And so I will go to the king, which is against the law; and if I perish, I perish!"

—Esther 4:13-16

The same Jesus Who turned water into wine can transform your home, your life, your family, and your future. He is still in the miracle-working business, and His business is the business of transformation.

—Adrian Rogers[1]

Do you ever worry about your future? Where will you go to college, will you get married, whom will you marry, will you have children, will your children be healthy, how will you pay the bills, how will you deal with this loss or that trial, where will you live, will your husband leave you, what will your health look like as you age, and the list of

1 http://christian-quotes.ochristian.com/christian-quotes_ochristian.cgi?query=future&action=Search&x=0&y=0, accessed September 24, 2019

worries can go on and on and on. Chances are you do worry about your future, at least from time to time. If so, you are in good company.

Before Queen Esther was Queen Esther, she was a young Jewish girl named Hadassah. Hadassah was an orphan living with her cousin, Mordecai, as a Jewish captive in Babylon. To make a long story short, the king at the time, King Ahasuerus, had banished his wife for having disregarded his wishes. This meant that the position of queen was open, and Ahasuerus went in search of someone new to become queen. The woman who ended up filling that position was none other than Hadassah, who then became known as Queen Esther. What the king did not know, however, was that Esther was a Jewish captive in his country.

To make things even more interesting, Ahasuerus had, as a member of his royal court, a man named Haman who hated Jews—in particular, Esther's cousin, Mordecai. Haman cooked up an evil scheme to do away with all the Jews in the country once and for all, which would, of necessity, also include Queen Esther if her identity as a Jewish woman were made known.

Queen Esther now found herself in an even more impossible situation than when she was first chosen to be queen (which was likely against her wishes). Now, she either had to keep silent and watch as Haman had her fellow Jews murdered, or else she had to speak up and risk her own life in doing so.

I encourage you to take the time to read the whole book of Esther and take in this epic story in its entirety, but suffice it to say that Esther put her neck on the line and not only approached the king (a capital offense if the king did not want to be approached), but also admitted to him that she was a Jew and knew of a plot to kill the Jewish people. God's favor was clearly with Queen Esther, and her being in a position to be able to be used to save the Jews was clearly a part of His amazing and perfect plan. And the same is true for you in whatever situation you find yourself right now, in this moment.

Perhaps you want to feel the hope and encouragement found in the powerful story of Queen Esther and God's using her to rescue the Jewish people. But perhaps your own circumstances seem too dire, too dark, too far removed from the glory and victory and joy of Queen Esther's uplifting testimony to God's goodness and faithfulness. Maybe you are in a dry wilderness season of the soul, and it is downright hard for you to believe you have a good future ahead of you.

May I remind you that the God of Esther is your God, too? He is the same yesterday, today, and forever and is in the business of redemption, rescue, and restoration. Jeremiah 29:11 is an incredibly popular verse these days. It says, "'For I know the thoughts that I think toward you.' says the Lord, 'thoughts of peace and not of evil, to give you a future and a hope.'" This is a beautiful passage of Scripture all on its own, but deprived of its context, it loses a bit of its luster and its rich meaning.

Jeremiah 29:10-14 says,

> For thus says the Lord: "After seventy years are completed at Babylon, I will visit you and perform My good word toward you, and cause you to return to this place. For I know the thoughts that I think toward you," says the Lord, "thoughts of peace and not of evil, to give you a future and a hope. Then you will call upon Me and go and pray to Me, and I will listen to you. And you will seek Me and find Me, when you search for Me with all your heart. I will be found by you," says the Lord, "and I will bring you back from your captivity; I will gather you from all the nations and from all the places where I have driven you", says the Lord, "and I will bring you to the place from which I cause you to be carried away captive."

Isn't that far more meaningful, especially when you are experiencing a hard time in your life? This Lenten season, don't view Jeremiah 29:11 as a Pollyanna-style verse that can't possibly apply to your current life situation. Instead, realize the context of the promise: the Jews were going through an incredibly hard time when the Lord issued forth to them this promise. They were in captivity, much as were the Jews of Esther's day. They had been taken away from their homeland. Things didn't look so hopeful for their future! And yet, with their faithful God, they could have hope.

They could have hope as long as they turned to Him in their trouble. If they sought His face in their hardship, they would find Him, and He would be faithful in His rescue and restoration of them and their situation—even though they had been terribly unfaithful to Him.

The same can be true for you, friend. If you are hurting today, if you are broken, if this Lenten season is a dark one for you, look to your Healer, your Rescuer, your Savior, the One in Whom you always have a future and a hope. He is there. And He will not let you down.

Action Step:

Take a piece of paper and make a list of all the areas of your life you are worried about right now, all the things that are going on (or that you are concerned might happen at some point), all the situations in which you feel you have no future and no hope. Now commit each of those areas in prayer to the Lord, laying them all down, one by one, at His feet. Finally, burn the peace of paper once you have done so and rest in Who you know Your God to be—your future and your hope.

Prayer:

Lord, life looks bleak. I can't see the forest for the trees in my life situation right now, and I often wonder how I can possibly have a future worth living on the other side of these trials. But I know Who Your Word says You are, and I am choosing today to do the hard thing—to stop my worry, stop my striving, and instead choose to believe and hope in that truth. Help me, Lord. Thank You for the good news that is always ever found in Your Word. In Jesus' name, Amen.

Day 19

Hannah and the Quest for Motherhood

So Hannah arose after they had finished eating and drinking in Shiloh. Now Eli the priest was sitting on the seat by the doorpost of the tabernacle of the Lord. And she was in bitterness of soul, and prayed to the Lord and wept in anguish. Then she made a vow and said, "O Lord of hosts, if You will indeed look on the affliction of Your maidservant and remember me, and not forget Your maidservant, but will give Your maidservant a male child, then I will give him to the Lord all the days of his life, and no razor shall come upon his head."

—1 Samuel 1:9-11

The motherhood to which every Christian woman is called is making disciples of all nations. We all must labor, prayerfully expectant that God will mercifully grant people new birth in Christ. Because Jesus is worthy to receive worship from the image bearers he has created, every human being is worthy of our labor and care in this endeavor of discipleship. In this sense there is no Christian woman who is child-free. We pass on the gospel to the next generation of worshipers, who will pass on the gospel to the next generation, and so on. The aim of our motherhood is to declare the good news to the next generation, "to a people yet unborn" (Ps. 22:31). We pass on the gospel because we know it is the only thing that will give our children the strength and motive to give their own lives in making disciples.

—Gloria Furman[1]

---

[1] https://www.goodreads.com/quotes/search?utf8=□&q=christian+motherhood&commit=Search, accessed September 24, 2019

Hannah felt the deep ache experienced by countless women down through history—the ache for a child of her own. She was one of the women caught in a two-wife marriage to a man named Elkanah. The other wife, Peninnah, had children of her own, but Hannah did not. Though Elkanah appears to have never berated her for this, the surrounding culture of the time no doubt did, for Hannah lived in a time wherein the worth and purpose of a woman was wrapped up in whether or not she could produce children, namely sons.

Sadly, this very concept is still around even today, though perhaps at least less common than it once was. Even today women are told that motherhood is the highest calling, implying that if you are single or married and childless, you have no purpose and little worth, for you are not fulfilling the highest calling on a woman's life. This damaging idea leads so many women to feelings of hurt, loss, despair, and purposelessness. Add to that the very normal and God-designed desire to have children of one's own, and the result is a mountain of pain and unmet desire in the hearts of women everywhere.

What I love about Hannah's example is that she didn't wallow in her despair. Neither did she go to God expressing the belief that if she were given a child, that child would be hers for the keeping. Instead, she went to God with her desire for a child of her own, while at the same time acknowledging that, truly, any child she was blessed with would ultimately belong to God first and foremost. This belief of Hannah's is illustrated in the promise she made to the Lord that if she were given a child, she would give him back to the Lord "all the days of his life."

And when the Lord grants her wish to become a mother? Hannah does not renege on her promise. First Samuel 1:21-28 says,

> Now the man Elkanah and all his house went up to offer to the Lord the yearly sacrifice and his vow. But Hannah did not go up, for she said to her husband, "Not until the child is weaned; then I will take him, that he may appear before the Lord and remain there forever." So Elkanah her husband said to her, "Do what seems best to you; wait until you have weaned him. Only let the Lord establish His word." Then the woman stayed and nursed her son until she had weaned him. Now when she had weaned him, she took him up with her, with three bulls, one ephah of flour, and a skin of wine, and brought him to the house of the Lord in Shiloh. And the child *was* young. Then they slaughtered a bull, and brought the child to Eli. And she said,

"O my lord! As your soul lives, my lord, I am the woman who stood by you here, praying to the Lord. For this child I prayed, and the Lord has granted me my petition which I asked of Him. Therefore I also have lent him to the Lord; as long as he lives he shall be lent to the Lord." So they worshiped the Lord there.

Can you imagine having to take the child for whom you yearned for so long to the house of the Lord and leaving him there? Many scholars say he would have been no older than about three when this occurred, and, from that point on, Hannah presumably only saw her son once a year, for 1 Samuel 2:18-19 says,

But Samuel ministered before the Lord, even as a child, wearing a linen ephod. Moreover his mother used to make him a little robe, and bring it to him year by year when she came up with her husband to offer the yearly sacrifice.

What a bittersweet thing that must have been for Hannah's mama heart.

While very few mothers leave their children at the age of three to be in the service of the Lord, the pain of wanting a child and not having one is, sadly, not a rare trial. Maybe it is one that you are in the middle of right now as you read these words. If that is true, I want to encourage your heart today.

This Lenten season, as you are yearning for a child and perhaps striving with all that you are and all that you have to make it happen, I want you to rest in some important truths today.

First, as enormous as is the blessing of a baby, no one—not even a sweet bundle of joy—can fill your heart or meet your deepest desires like God. Have you wondered before how Hannah was able to leave behind her little son and still go on? It is because she delighted in the Lord first and foremost and found her ultimate fulfillment in Him. First Samuel 2:1-2 says,

And Hannah prayed and said: "My heart rejoices in the Lord; My horn is exalted in the Lord. I smile at my enemies, because I rejoice in Your salvation. No one is holy like the Lord, for there is none besides You, nor is there any rock like our God."

Children are a gift and bring with them so much joy. But ultimately, we cannot look to them to be our source of fulfillment, identity, or joy. That has to be found in God alone.

Second, even if you never become a mama of your own children, as Gloria Furman points out in the quote above, you are called to and able to be a spiritual mother. In fact, that is your life's mission and purpose as someone called to fulfill the Great Commission. That is your highest calling—to serve as Christ's ambassador. Paul never had any children of his own, either, but he sure did have countless spiritual children! He even alludes to this concept of spiritual parenting in both 1 and 2 Timothy. First Timothy 1:1-2a says, "Paul, an apostle of Jesus Christ, by the commandment of God our Savior and the Lord Jesus Christ, our hope, to Timothy, a true son in the faith." Second Timothy begins much the same way: "Paul, an apostle of Jesus Christ by the will of God, according to the promise of life which is in Christ Jesus, to Timothy, a beloved son" (2 Timothy 1:1-2a).

Rest assured, sweet friend, that even if you never have children of your own, you can and should have spiritual children in numbers far exceeding what you could have biologically. Don't strive for motherhood, don't strive for purpose, don't work yourself to the bone trying to make your life count. It already does. Just as you are, as a child of God who is seeking to love and honor Him with all she does, you are already living a life of impact for the kingdom. Never forget that.

Action Step:

Write down a list of young women you could reach out to in the hope of mothering them in the faith. Seek to be a mentor, and you will never be at a loss for lives to impact for God's kingdom.

Prayer:

Lord, I thank You that none of the cultural lies about a woman and her purpose in this life have a hold over me. No one is allowed to define me and my identity except You, the One Who made me and has a whole lifetime of good works already prepared for me to walk in. Thank You that You see me as Your beloved daughter and not just as someone who can or should have children. My worth is in You, not what I do. And I thank You for that. Help me to rest in that truth this Lenten season and throughout the rest of my life. In Jesus' name, Amen.

Day 20

Pharaoh's Daughter and the Quest for a Rescue

Then the daughter of Pharaoh came down to bathe at the river. And her maidens walked along the riverside; and when she saw the ark among the reeds, she sent her maid to get it. And when she opened it, she saw the child, and behold, the baby wept. So she had compassion on him, and said, "This is one of the Hebrews' children." Then his sister said to Pharaoh's daughter, "Shall I go and call a nurse for you from the Hebrew women, that she may nurse the child for you?" And Pharaoh's daughter said to her, "Go." So the maiden went and called the child's mother. Then Pharaoh's daughter said to her, "Take this child away and nurse him for me, and I will give you your wages." So the woman took the child and nursed him. And the child grew, and she brought him to Pharaoh's daughter, and he became her son. So she called his name Moses, saying, "Because I drew him out of the water."

—Exodus 2:5-10

The Bible is one long story of God meeting our rebellion with His rescue, our sin with His salvation, our guilt with His grace, our badness with His goodness. The overwhelming focus of the Bible is not the work of the redeemed but the work of the Redeemer. Which means that the Bible is not first a recipe for Christian living but a revelation book of Jesus who is the answer to our un-Christian living.

—Tullian Tchividjian[1]

1 https://www.goodreads.com/quotes/search?commit=Search&page=2&q=god+rescue&u tf8=□, accessed September 24, 2019

If you think about it, Pharaoh's daughter was an incredibly bold, principled, fearless woman. Here she was, the daughter of the reigning leader of all Egypt at the time, and she intentionally and willfully went against his wrongful decree. Because he feared that the Hebrews' ever-increasing population would lead to their outnumbering his own people and would therefore lead to their overthrowing his rule, Pharaoh had ordered that all baby boys born to the Hebrews be killed upon birth.

One such baby, Moses, had a birth mother who refused to give up on him. His mother also had two midwives who refused to murder the baby they had just delivered into the world. And after his birth mother sent him down the Nile in a little basket with the hope that he would be safe from Pharaoh's decree, Pharaoh's own daughter became another female hero in Moses' life story.

For years I never thought about the bravery which would have been required for Pharaoh's daughter to do this. To rescue the baby and decide to bring him up as her own at a time when her father surely could have deciphered that this was a Hebrew baby was quite the daring move! But as full of dire consequences as her actions could have been, she nevertheless chose to do what she knew was right—she rescued the little baby.

No doubt Moses' birth mother thought his situation looked dire and hopeless. Though she had concealed his existence from the Egyptians as long as she could following his birth, the day nevertheless came when she knew she must relinquish him into God's hands and hope for the best. As a mother myself, I can only imagine the anxiety she must have experienced as she hoped and prayed for rescue for her son but feared there would be none.

If there is something this amazing story shows us, however, it is that Moses' God is a God of rescue. He had a plan for that little baby's life, even in the midst of incredibly dark and terrible circumstances. All along He had a plan that would involve this baby growing up to become the one whom God would use to rescue His people from their years-long enslavement under Pharaoh. It didn't make sense to Moses' mother how things could possibly work out, but they did—because our God is a God of rescue.

The same is true for where He has you—right here, right now, in this Lenten season. I don't know what your current life circumstances look like. I don't know what you are in need of being rescued from. I have no idea. But God does. And He hasn't fallen asleep at the wheel. He hasn't forgotten about you. And He certainly isn't chomping His proverbial fingernails trying to figure out what He is going to do about your situation and how on earth He is going to come to your rescue.

Whatever you are experiencing, God's got this. He's got you. And your rescuer and helper will not tarry, will not delay, and will not forsake you in your pain and in your trial. Psalm 18:1-3 says:

> I will love You, O Lord, my strength. The Lord is my rock and my fortress and my deliverer; My God, my strength, in whom I will trust; My shield and the horn of my salvation, my stronghold. I will call upon the Lord, *who is worthy* to be praised; So shall I be saved from my enemies.

This was true for David, and it is true for you, too. Do you need rescued today? Are you striving to find hope, to discover answers, to know what to do in this unbearably dark season? Look to the Lord. He is your Rescuer. You need only to rest in Him, ceasing from your striving and worry. "For thus says the Lord God, the Holy One of Israel: 'In returning and rest you shall be saved; In quietness and confidence shall be your strength'" (Isaiah 30:15a).

Action Step:

Read more of Moses' story as found in the book of Exodus and watch your faith be built up as you realize how Romans 8:28 (that God brings good out of everything that happens in the lives of His people) has been true throughout all of time and is still true for you, even today.

Prayer:

Lord, You know what I'm going through. Maybe not many people do, but You do. And You know I need a rescue. I'm drowning here and searching desperately for a way out. Help me to rely on and trust in You as my rescuer. Help me to believe that the amazing things You did for others You are still capable of doing now. Thank You for Your dedication to bring good out of everything that happens in my life, and may that truth bring me comfort and strength in the days ahead. In Jesus' name, Amen.

Day 21

The Proverbs 31 Woman and the Quest for Calling

She watches over the ways of her household, and does not eat the bread of idleness. Her children rise up and call her blessed; Her husband also, and he praises her: "Many daughters have done well, but you excel them all." Charm is deceitful and beauty is passing, but a woman who fears the Lord, she shall be praised. Give her of the fruit of her hands, and let her own works praise her in the gates.

—Proverbs 31:27-31

Some evangelicals have turned Proverbs 31 into a woman's job description instead of what it actually is: the blessing and affirmation of valor for the lives of women, memorized by Jewish husbands for the purpose of honoring their wives at the family table. It is meant as a celebration for the everyday moments of valor for everyday women, not as an impossible exhausting standard.

—Sarah Bessey[1]

If there is a woman in the Bible whose example would tempt us to remain in striving mode, it would be this lady right here. We read Proverbs 31:10-31 and begin making mental notes, listing all the many tasks this lady performs day in and day out: She does her husband good, seeks wool and flax and works as an excellent seamstress, gathers food from afar, rises while it is yet night and assigns jobs to her

1 https://www.goodreads.com/quotes/search?utf8=□&q=proverbs+31&commit=Search, accessed September 26, 2019

maidservants, considers a field and buys it, makes money by planting vineyards, builds up her strength, produces good merchandise, serves the poor, clothes her household in only the finest, makes and sells linen garments and sashes, speaks with wisdom and kindness, watches over her household, and fears the Lord.

Quite a long laundry list, right? You may be wondering at this point how she has time to do all those things and how you are going to make it work to accomplish the same long list of tasks each and every day in order to please God and be a "biblical woman."

But that's just it—that isn't at all what God expects of you. And the "Proverbs 31 woman" isn't even one real woman! Rather, she is a description presented by a mother to her son (see Proverbs 31:1) of what a God-fearing woman might accomplish in her life and what her character might look like. It is showing that to be a truly biblical woman, one must fear the Lord, for everything else flows from that heart posture. It is showing myriad different ways in which women can bring glory to God by being productive, loving, caring, servant-hearted workers, mothers, wives, bosses, and women in general.

Women can serve the poor, bring up children, be competent wives, live as excellent home managers, run their own businesses, and teach truth to others. But that doesn't at all mean that God is expecting women to do all of these things, all at the same time. Instead, this passage shows a picture of how different women can bring glory and honor to God and impact His kingdom, as well as a picture of what one woman might do all throughout her life, in and out of different seasons. But what Proverbs 31 truly all boils down to is this: where your heart is as a woman, and whether or not fearing and following God is your primary concern.

It isn't about crossing everything off your to-do list, striving around the clock, doing "all the things," one-upping other women, being "Pinterest perfect," ministering to everyone you possibly can, meeting every need out there, and working yourself to the bone. It's about fearing the Lord, loving Him, and allowing that relationship with Him to drive and inspire every single other thing you do with your life.

Because you know what? That is exactly how Jesus lived—in step with the Father. He didn't meet every need, heal every person, answer every question, or teach every multitude that came His way. Sometimes, right at the very moment when the multitude was coming after Him and searching for Him, was precisely when Jesus chose to withdraw from the crowds and their needs, questions, and concerns.

It was in those very moments that He chose to go off and be with the Father and commune with Him in prayer. It wasn't that Christ didn't have a heart for the masses. He clearly did! But He also knew where His first priority lay, and He also knew that spending that time with the Father was what bolstered Him for His everyday work and ministry.

How much better off we would all be if we, too, understood that! Too often, we're too busy running around like the proverbial chicken with its head cut off, striving for purpose, chasing after "calling," trying to decipher what is our calling, and then hustling to make it happen. All we truly need to do, though, is keep in step with the Father. We need to remember who we are in Him: image bearers of God, ambassadors of Christ, and those tasked with carrying out the Great Commission.

In order to fulfill those roles, however, this Lenten season we must truly seek to emulate how Christ lived. And that means not only serving people or working hard, but also withdrawing at times, too, refusing to strive, rejecting the "hustle" mentality, and keeping our eyes fixed on the Father to see what is and what is not our calling, role, and responsibility in this season.

This will feel counterintuitive; it will be hard. And it certainly won't appear appropriate to the culture around us. But it will be worth it, it will be God-honoring, and it will be crucial for our ongoing ability to live a sustainable life full of rest and work, ministry and prayer, service and solitude. Make this your aim this Lenten season, and the peace of God will fill your heart as perhaps never before.

Action Step:

Ask the Lord to show you what being a Proverbs 31 woman looks like for you personally right here, right now, in this season. And then be willing to heed whatever it is that He says to you, refusing to compare yourself to anyone else.

Prayer:

Lord, help me to reorient my thinking surrounding the Proverbs 31 woman and what that passage of Scripture means for my life. For too long I have bought into the lie that to be a godly woman living out biblical womanhood, I have to strive, hustle, and work myself to the bone. Thank You for showing me that rest is not sinful, that withdrawing is not selfish, and that, sometimes, that is the best thing I can do. Help me to walk in Your steps, Lord. In Jesus' name, Amen.

Day 22

Miriam and the Quest for Rejoicing

Then Miriam the prophetess, the sister of Aaron, took the timbrel in her hand; and all the women went out after her with timbrels and with dances. And Miriam answered them: "Sing to the Lord, for He has triumphed gloriously! The horse and its rider He has thrown into the sea!"

—Exodus 15:20-21

When was the last time you laughed for the sheer joy of your salvation? People are not attracted to somber doctrines. There is no persuasive power in a gloomy and morbid religion. Let the world see your joy and you won't be able to keep them away. To be filled with God is to be filled with joy.

—Author Unknown[1]

Miriam lived in a most interesting era, experiencing some incredibly hard yet also incredibly powerful events. She was Moses' sister and the one who kept a close eye on him when their mother sent baby Moses down the Nile River. Exodus 2:7 says, "Then his sister said to Pharaoh's daughter, 'Shall I go and call a nurse for you from the Hebrew women, that she may nurse the child for you?'" Not only did Miriam keep an eye out for what would happen to Moses as he floated away on the Nile, but she was also the one responsible for arranging it to where Moses' own biological mother could be the one to nurse the baby for Pharaoh's daughter.

1 https://www.viralbeliever.com/christian-quotes-about-joy/, accessed September 28, 2019

As if living in this time of slavery, intrigue, danger, and hardship were not enough excitement for one young girl, Miriam was also present for God's amazing and miraculous acts of deliverance on behalf of the Hebrew people. After the onslaught of the ten plagues, Pharaoh finally chose to release the Hebrews from their years-long stint in slavery. But just as they were traveling on their way to freedom, he changed his mind yet again. He decided he wanted the Hebrews back under his thumb and followed them as they tried to make their journey into a new life.

Exodus 14:5-27 says,

> Now it was told the king of Egypt that the people had fled, and the heart of Pharaoh and his servants was turned against the people; and they said, "Why have we done this, that we have let Israel go from serving us?" So he made ready his chariot and took his people with him. Also, he took six hundred choice chariots, and all the chariots of Egypt with captains over every one of them. And the Lord hardened the heart of Pharaoh king of Egypt, and he pursued the children of Israel; and the children of Israel went out with boldness. So the Egyptians pursued them, all the horses and chariots of Pharaoh, his horsemen and his army, and overtook them camping by the sea beside Pi Hahiroth, before Baal Zephon. And when Pharaoh drew near, the children of Israel lifted their eyes, and behold, the Egyptians marched after them. So they were very afraid, and the children of Israel cried out to the Lord. Then they said to Moses, "Because there were no graves in Egypt, have you taken us away to die in the wilderness? Why have you so dealt with us, to bring us up out of Egypt? Is this not the word that we told you in Egypt, saying, 'Let us alone that we may serve the Egyptians?' For it would have been better for us to serve the Egyptians than that we should die in the wilderness."

> And Moses said to the people, "Do not be afraid. Stand still, and see the salvation of the Lord, which He will accomplish for you today. For the Egyptians whom you see today, you shall see again no more forever. The Lord will fight for you, and you shall hold your peace." And the Lord said to Moses, "Why do you cry to Me? Tell the children of Israel to go forward. But lift up your rod, and stretch out your hand over the sea and divide it. And

the children of Israel shall go on dry ground through the midst of the sea. And I indeed will harden the hearts of the Egyptians, and they shall follow them. So I will gain honor over Pharaoh and over all his army, his chariots, and his horsemen. Then the Egyptians shall know that I am the Lord, when I have gained honor for Myself over Pharaoh, his chariots, and his horsemen." And the Angel of God, who went before the camp of Israel, moved and went behind them; and the pillar of cloud went from before them and stood behind them. So it came between the camp of the Egyptians and the camp of Israel. Thus it was a cloud and darkness to the one, and it gave light by night to the other, so that the one did not come near the other all that night. Then Moses stretched out his hand over the sea; and the Lord caused the sea to go back by a strong east wind all that night, and made the sea into dry land, and the waters were divided. So the children of Israel went into the midst of the sea on the dry ground, and the waters were a wall to them on their right hand and on their left.

And the Egyptians pursued and went after them into the midst of the sea, all Pharaoh's horses, his chariots, and his horsemen. Now it came to pass, in the morning watch, that the Lord looked down upon the army of the Egyptians through the pillar of fire and cloud, and He troubled the army of the Egyptians. And He took off their chariot wheels, so that they drove them with difficulty; and the Egyptians said, "Let us flee from the face of Israel, for the Lord fights for them against the Egyptians." Then the Lord said to Moses, "Stretch out your hand over the sea, that the waters may come back upon the Egyptians, on their chariots, and on their horsemen." And Moses stretched out his hand over the sea; and when the morning appeared, the sea returned to its full depth, while the Egyptians were fleeing into it. So the Lord overthrew the Egyptians in the midst of the sea.

It is upon this amazing rescue that Miriam, now a prophetess, rejoices, dances, and proclaims the truth in song. (The words of her song are quoted in the passage at the beginning of this section.) She truly had seen God come to the rescue of her people in the midst of what appeared to be a hopeless situation.

Though life is rarely ever perfectly easy, trouble free, and devoid of pain and heartache, we can nevertheless always rejoice because our God always has a plan—and a good one at that! As the prophet Jeremiah pointed out in Jeremiah 29, God always has thoughts of hope and a future for His people, even when they are in the direst of circumstances (see verses 10-14). Whatever you currently may be experiencing, whatever you may have struggled through in the past, and whatever may come your way in the future, there is still always a reason and a call to rejoice, for your God loves you, wants what is ultimately best for you, and always has your best interests in mind.

You don't have to strive to rejoice in the hard times. All you have to do is fix your eyes on your God. The rest will follow as you remember His goodness and His faithfulness in the past that will also be yours in the future.

Action Step:

Take out a piece of paper and begin to list all the various reasons you have to rejoice right now, right where you are. Count your blessings, recount the ways God has proven Himself faithful in the past, and remember the ways He has tangibly revealed His love for you all throughout your life. Return again and again to this list as needed, also adding to it in the years to come.

Prayer:

Lord, help me not to fix my eyes on my problems, but rather on Your Word, Your character, and Your promises. Help me to remember that they aren't just for some random group of people somewhere, but that they are actually for me, today and every day, as Your beloved daughter. Thank You for Your love, Lord, and for the many reasons I have to rejoice. In Jesus' name, Amen

Day 23

Elizabeth and the Quest for Joy

Now after those days his wife Elizabeth conceived; and she hid herself five months, saying, "Thus the Lord has dealt with me, in the days when He looked on me, to take away my reproach among people."

—Luke 1:24-25

Begin to rejoice in the Lord, and your bones will flourish like an herb, and your cheeks will glow with the bloom of health and freshness. Worry, fear, distrust, care—all are poisonous! Joy is balm and healing, and if you will but rejoice, God will give power.

—A.B. Simpson[1]

"To treat a person as insignificant or peripheral"[2]...that is what it means to "marginalize" someone.[3] I can think of many marginalized people in the Word, all of whom were the very ones Christ sought. He repeatedly said He did not come for the well-off, self-righteous, prideful, judgmental folk (such as the Pharisees, Mark 2:16-17). He came for the poor, the destitute, the sinful, the lost, the mistreated, the tax collector, the prostitute, the woman, the childless, the blind man, and so many more. The ones whom society marginalized, the ones the culture viewed as insignificant, the ones only good for being on the peripheral of society—He came for *those* people.

---

1 http://christian-quotes.ochristian.com/christian-quotes_ochristian.cgi?query=joy&action=Search&x=0&y=0, accessed September 14, 2019

2 https://en.oxforddictionaries.com/definition/us/marginalize ... accessed September 27, 2018

3 A portion of this section first appeared in Rebekah Hargraves, *Good News for a Woman's Heart: An Advent Devotional Study* (Rebekah Hargraves: 2018)

And yet, ironically, we as His followers oftentimes act more like the Pharisees toward these very people than like Christ Himself, the One whose ambassadors, hands, and feet we have been commissioned to be.

If we are only surrounding ourselves with people who look, act, think, and live just like we do, then something is wrong. A portion of our call and purpose to be Great Commission workers is being ignored. For many of us, the only friends and community we have consists of all like-minded Christian believers. And while this is incredibly important on so many levels—after all, we were never meant to walk through life alone without friends who would be as iron that sharpens iron (Proverbs 27:17)—this isn't all there is to living the Christian life.

We need the encouragement, edification, and camaraderie which come through cultivating growing friendships with believers, but these friendships are not an end in and of themselves; they are a means to an end. They not only contribute to our ongoing growth and sanctification, but they also help equip us to actually go out and fulfill the Great Commission with regard to the unbelievers on our street and in our community.

God never intended for us to remain holed up in our churches and Christian groups. Those are the basic training centers—the places where we are trained to then go out and love others well in both word and deed. The church is not the end; it's the means to the end of spreading the truth and being the salt and light this world needs. If we are only living life with like-minded friends, we actually aren't doing the Christian life very well at all.

What we need to be doing is going out in the community to seek those who have been marginalized—the ones who are made to feel as if they are "less-than" in one way or another or who may not feel comfortable stepping foot into some of our churches, where they may be made to feel as if they just aren't "good enough" (as if we aren't all in desperate need of God's grace ourselves!). What we need to be doing is being the true hands and feet of Christ, as if it is that for which we were given time...because it is!

I see Elizabeth as a beautiful example of a marginalized life forever changed through the love and grace of our merciful God. She went from being the victim of the reproach of people in her community to being reminded of the fact—in a very tangible way—that God really did always love her and never had forgotten about her and her heart.

Another beautiful example of a marginalized woman being reached out to, loved by God, and given great joy in the process is the Samaritan woman Jesus met at the well in John 4. To grasp just how revolutionary this action of Christ's would have been, consider for a moment the long and checkered past between the Jews and the Samaritans. Here is an excerpt from an article I wrote last year on this topic:

By the time Jesus arrived at the well, the Jews had endured an age-long struggle with the Samaritan people, which had finally culminated in the Jews not even being willing to speak to anyone of Samaritan descent (John 4:9). We see this ancient trouble beginning to brew all the way back in 2 Kings 17:24-28, when people of all different nations and backgrounds were placed in the land of Samaria, which had first belonged to the Jews. Before long, these foreigners began to intermarry with the Jewish people, and because they served false gods, their children were raised in a mixed-faith culture blending Jewish beliefs and traditions with rampant false religious teachings. Trouble between the two cultures continued to escalate as the Samaritans then sought to halt the Jews' project of rebuilding Jerusalem's walls (Nehemiah 6:1-14).

The Jews' continued hatred toward the Samaritans becomes quite evident in the New Testament, when we discover that Jews didn't even speak to Samaritans (John 4:9). Imagine the surprise (and outrage!) of the Jewish people when Jesus not only spoke to Samaritans, treating them as equal to the Jews, but even went so far as to make a Samaritan the "good guy hero" of one of His stories!

This would have seemed completely outlandish and inappropriate. But Jesus did it anyway, and I'm glad He did! He taught us a valuable lesson which is oh-so-relevant to today.[4]

Unfortunately, this kind of behavior still goes on today; we still battle it. We want to be in the world but not of it (John 17:16), but we have forgotten what that even means. What that phrase really means is that we are to be eternally minded, seeking to have the mind of Christ and walking by the Spirit in unity with the Lord. It means we are mindful of the fact that we are strangers in this world, and that this world is not our home. It means that, because we are citizens of heaven, we seek to take the way life will be then and infuse it into the now of everyday

---

4 This section first appeared in a blog post I wrote - http://www.gracefullytruthful.com/author/rhargravesgt700/ , accessed September 27, 2018

life. There is love there, so we seek to be loving here; there is holiness there, so we seek to be holy here. What it does not mean is that you never go near the people of this world for fear that their "worldliness" will spread as a contagion to you.

The sobering reality is that if we are not seeking to love, reach out to, encourage, practice hospitality with, minister to, and point to Christ the lost people of the world, then we are failing as Great Commission workers.

It is our call as Christ followers to welcome the outcast.

It is our call as Christ followers to include the marginalized.

Just like Christ did.

And you know what is so beautiful about all this? I cannot think of a more apt or wonderful time to begin to do so than right now during this wonderful season of Lent—the season in which we commemorate and celebrate what Christ did for us on the cross.

Before we close for today and you go shopping for that Easter dress or for goodies with which to fill your children's Easter baskets, I want to speak to those of you who may be the marginalized or forgotten this season.

Maybe you are a recently widowed mama who is trying to keep it all together but feeling so left out as you see all the sweet matching and coordinating family Easter outfits in sales ads. Perhaps you are a military wife whose husband is currently deployed, and this Lenten season is incredibly painful for you. Maybe you (like many others, as you aren't alone!) have a checkered past and have been subconsciously made to feel as if you have to be "perfect" in order to "fit in" in the church. Maybe you're the new girl in your town or church or workplace and have no friends with whom to celebrate the season. Whatever your situation, you are on a quest for joy and finding it nowhere.

Whatever your circumstances may be, I want you to know something: The same God who worked a miracle in the life and heart of Elizabeth is the same God who wants to do the same in your life. The same Jesus who willingly reached out to and spoke with a hated, judged, mistreated, hurting Samaritan woman is the same Jesus who is able to save you from your past and gift you with His love, His holiness, and His perfection. The same Jesus who felt so alone and betrayed on the cross is the same Jesus who understands your pain and wants to enfold you in His love. Our God is the same yesterday, today, and forever, and the character He manifested in the Word is the same character He has toward you today. Delight in His love for you and allow it to bring you great joy this Lent.

Action Step:

Get out a piece of paper and write down five things for which you are thankful today. Then flip the piece of paper over and make a list of five people you could reach out to today with whom you can spread the joy of Christ. Then act on that list. Send an encouraging text, drop off a surprise cup of coffee on that friend's front porch, or offer to babysit that mama's little ones so she can have some time to herself. Whatever you do, make it your aim to get away from the distractions and live on mission in light of the joy you have been given in Christ.

Prayer:

Lord, thank You for Your heart for me. Thank You for all You have done in my life to afford me grace, forgiveness, love, peace, and joy. Thank You that I don't have to strive for a "perfect" life with "perfect" circumstances in order to have joy. Help me to daily remember that all I have to do is fix my eyes on You—my Father, Defender, Friend, and Savior. In Jesus' name, Amen.

Day 24

Mary and the Quest for Purpose

"Behold the maidservant of the Lord! Let it be to me according to your word."

—Luke 1:38

May not a single moment of my life be spent outside the light, love and joy of God's presence and not a moment without the entire surrender of myself as a vessel for Him to fill full of His Spirit and His love.

—Andrew Murray[1]

Now we come to the story of Mary,[2] the mother of Jesus, the fifth and final woman listed in His genealogy. When I read her story each Christmas season, what strikes me the most is seeing the hope that was brought to all mankind through her willingness to surrender to the Father's will.

Scholars often say that she was likely no more than about fourteen years of age when she was visited by the angel and told she was going to give birth to a son. Fourteen! We read the amazing story of Mary's willing surrender to the Father's will in the narrative Luke writes in Luke 1:26-38.

What amazes me the most is that, apart from her initial shock over how it could be that she, a virgin, could bear a son, Mary immediately jumps to surrender and obedience. We read her words in Luke 1:38,

1 http://christian-quotes.ochristian.com/christian-quotes_ochristian.cgi?query=surrender&action=Search&x=0&y=0, accessed September 14th, 2019

2 A portion of this section first appeared in Rebekah Hargraves, *Good News for a Woman's Heart: An Advent Devotional Study* (Rebekah Hargraves: 2018)

"Behold the maidservant of the Lord! Let it be to me according to your word." She describes herself as a servant of the Lord; she has no agenda of her own but rather finds her purpose and mission in doing her Master's bidding. Such is the kind of heartfelt response we find in Luke 1. No grumbling, no trying to find a way out, no argument, no frustration or anger or pride, nothing. Simply quiet, willing surrender. To say that she possessed an amazing sense of faithfulness for a young teen would be an understatement!

Mary's faithfulness *to* God was the natural outworking of her faith *in* God. We read, in what has become known as Mary's Magnificat (Song of Mary), of this young girl in Luke 1:46-55 singing forth a hymn of praise to her God. This song is a staggering and countercultural portrayal of Mary's theological prowess in a day and age in which women and girls were not regularly taught theology. This theological training, however, was a godsend, for it was precisely what prepared her for the hard work to which God had called her. Had she not known her theology and had she not known God to be a God of goodness, love, mercy, and compassion, she never could have willingly and trustfully surrendered herself to her Master's bidding in the way that she did.

God's call on Mary's life was definitely a hard one. Remember, she is likely in her early teens as all of this is happening. She is betrothed to Joseph, but they have not yet come together intimately. She is living as a young girl in a culture and under an old covenant in which women and girls were regularly stoned to death for not being virgins when they married (see Deuteronomy 22:13-22). Mary is agreeing to what could potentially be a death sentence for her. And yet, her faith and trust in (not to mention her evident love for) her Lord renders her willing and able to surrender whatever plan she may have had for her own life so that she can instead take on the plan prepared for her beforehand by the hand of her Heavenly Father. She exhibits great strength and fortitude in the face of a call which would leave many a weaker woman trembling off in a corner somewhere. God not only called her to this mission, but in His grace He also strengthened and equipped her for it.

Truly, it was her willingness to follow the Lord and His mission for her life and the surrendering of her body as a willing vessel for the world-changing plan of the Lord which secured for us the hope we each so desperately crave as we live out our days in this sin-cursed world. Granted, if Mary had not willingly submitted to the Lord's overarching plan for her life, He would have found someone else who would in order for His great plan of redemption to unfold as first prophesied all the way back in the garden (Genesis 3:14-15). But He didn't have to. Mary knew Him, and that is what made her willing to follow Him.

That, my friend, is why we are able to have hope today—an unending, unfaltering, persevering hope in the face of even the worst of life's trials and hardships.

Today, as we consider Mary's actions, I pray you walk away feeling refreshed, renewed, and infused with a new sense of hope. A hope you can take with you as you journey through the rest of this Lenten season and on into the rest of the year. A hope that the enemy can't shake. A hope that is not based on your circumstances, your background, your age, your bank account, your family situation, your friendships (or lack thereof), your past (or present) sins and failures, or anything else you could imagine. I am praying for you a hope that is unchanging specifically because it is not based on the changing realities of your day-to-day life. Rather, I pray that you will be able to journey forth from this study feeling within you a tangible hope that can only come from our great Lord and Savior, Jesus Christ Himself. The same Christ who intentionally and graciously included women with rather colorful and challenging stories and backgrounds in His genealogy. The same Christ Who desires to do that very thing for you today as He welcomes you into His forever family.

While we pause this season from all the stress and overwhelm of our typical daily schedules and seek to step back from the many distractions, may we remember this: We don't have to strive to find our purpose. We don't have to think that living a life of purpose for the kingdom requires that we always be rushing to and fro, running on empty. This is not at all that for which God designed us! Jesus said in Matthew 11:28-30,

> "Come to Me, all you who labor and are heavy laden, and I will give you rest. Take My yoke upon you and learn from Me, for I am gentle and lowly in heart, and you will find rest for your souls. For My yoke is easy and My burden is light."

Paul writes in Ephesians 2:10, "For we are His workmanship, created in Christ Jesus for good works, which God prepared beforehand that we should walk in them." We don't have to push, strive, and overextend ourselves in order to live a life of impact. All we need to do is keep in step with the Spirit and follow Him as He leads. After all, those good works He designed for us to walk in were prepared for us before we ever even came to be.

Action Step:

Spend some time with the Lord today assessing your daily to-do list and schedule in light of His plan for your life. Does He really want you thinking you have to do everything which is currently a part of your days and weeks? Or are there things you are regularly doing in an effort to find purpose that are actually hindering your ability to be free to do those things which He truly has called you to do?

Prayer:

Lord, show me what I am missing. Show me where I am wrongly thinking my purpose lies, and help me to see clearly to know what Your purpose is for my life in this current season, with these current life circumstances. You promised in James 1:5 to generously give me wisdom when I ask for it, and I trust You, knowing that You will bring this promise to pass in my life. Thank You in advance for what You will show me and how it will reduce my overwhelm when I am moving to the tempo of your plan. In Jesus' name, Amen.

Day 25

Anna and the Quest for Prophecies Fulfilled

Now there was one, Anna, a prophetess, the daughter of Phanuel, of the tribe of Asher. She was of a great age, and had lived with a husband seven years from her virginity; and this woman was a widow of about eighty-four years, who did not depart from the temple, but served God with fastings and prayers night and day. And coming in that instant she gave thanks to the Lord, and spoke of Him to all those who looked for redemption in Jerusalem.

—Luke 2:36-38

God has wisely kept us in the dark concerning future events and reserved for himself the knowledge of them, that he may train us up in a dependence upon himself and a continued readiness for every event.

—Matthew Henry[1]

I love the story of Anna. Had I not already had a Grandma named Anna after whom I wanted to name my firstborn daughter, I may have still chosen that name just by nature of the fact that the prophetess Anna is such a neat example to us of a woman who lived a life of such joy, hope, purpose, impact, and love for God, even in the midst of very young widowhood, childlessness, and a life spent largely alone in the temple day in and day out.

1 https://www.christianquotes.info/quotes-by-topic/quotes-about-prophecy/, accessed September 26, 2019

In a culture in which a woman's worth would have been based on whether or not she was married and a mother, Anna's example stands out in contradiction to that myth of where a woman's worth actually lies. Here was a woman whose faith in God was what constituted her identity and made her life a fruitful one—not her marital status.

Anna had married quite young (as was the custom of the time), with many girls marrying at ages as young as twelve or thirteen. She had been married for seven years when her husband died, leaving her a bereft widow. Rather than remarrying as would have been common, Anna instead lived out her days as a widow in the temple of God. She was a prophetess in every sense of the word, daily serving God through fasting and prayer. But even more than that, after she came face to face with the promised Child, she also proclaimed the truth of God to all those who were looking for the long-awaited Messiah.

This clearly implies that she did not proclaim the reality of the prophecies she was seeing fulfilled right before her very eyes only to women. No, she proclaimed God's truth to men, as well, much as did Deborah, Huldah, Priscilla, and Mary Magdalene. Throughout the Bible we see women being faithful to teach everyone—men and women alike—the good news of God's Word, and the prophetess Anna was no exception.

Anna had waited quite a long time to see the prophecy of the coming Messiah fulfilled, but it was finally fulfilled. Maybe you, too, are waiting for certain prophecies to be fulfilled, and you are starting to lose hope by nature of just how long it is taking for these things to play out in your life. Maybe you have suffered great losses in your life, and you are just ready for the second coming of Christ to finally happen. Maybe you have many family members and friends awaiting you in Heaven, and you are so ready to see the end times prophecies fulfilled. Life has been hard for you, and you are ready for the Lord to tarry no longer.

Or perhaps you look at a promise such as the one found in Romans 8:28—"And we know that all things work together for good to those who love God, to those who are the called according to His purpose"—and your heart is yearning more than anything for good to be seen coming from the terrible life circumstances you have been through lately. You want to see prophecies and promises fulfilled, but you just aren't seeing it. May I encourage you today with the words of Peter in 2 Peter 3?

Beloved, I now write to you this second epistle (in both of which I stir up your pure minds by way of reminder), that you may be mindful of the words which were spoken before by the holy prophets, and of the commandment of us, the apostles of the Lord and Savior, knowing this first: that scoffers will come in the last days, walking according to their own lusts, and saying, "Where is the promise of His coming? For since the fathers fell asleep, all things continue as they were from the beginning of creation." For this they willfully forget: that by the word of God the heavens were of old, and the earth standing out of water and in the water, by which the world that then existed perished, being flooded with water. But the heavens and the earth which are now preserved by the same word, are reserved for fire until the day of judgment and perdition of ungodly men. But, beloved, do not forget this one thing, that with the Lord one day is as a thousand years, and a thousand years as one day. The Lord is not slack concerning His promise, as some count slackness, but is longsuffering toward us, not willing that any should perish but that all should come to repentance (2 Peter 3:1-9).

It may seem as if the Lord is dragging His proverbial heels but know this: It's for a good reason that the Lord tarries. As concerning His second coming, He has not returned yet in order to give people more time to turn from their sinful ways and trust in Him as their Savior. His heart is filled with love for them, and that is why we have not yet seen Him face to face, though we long to. His heart is ever concerned with His children and those who will one day come to Him and be His.

So, friend, this Lenten season, do not give in to despair. God hasn't forgotten you. He has not reneged on His promises; He will yet fulfill them—if not in this life, most certainly in the next. Hold fast to the encouraging words of Romans 8:18, "For I consider that the sufferings of this present time are not worthy to be compared with the glory which shall be revealed in us." Once we see our Savior face to face, all the pain and heartache we faced in this life will be seen as having been well worth it.

Action Step:

Take your fears, your heart cries, your desperation for promises fulfilled to the Lord today. Lay them all at His feet. And consider picking up a wonderful book written by my friend, Glenna Marshall, entitled *The Promise is His Presence: Why God is Always Enough*. It will be a balm to your soul.

Prayer:

Lord, You know how I long to see You. You know how dark and heart-wrenching and downright tiresome this life can be sometimes. I ask now that You help me to look not to what You might promise me but to You Yourself, for You are worth infinitely more than whatever gift or blessing You could offer. Help me to believe and remember that Your timing is perfect, and I can rest in it. In Jesus' name, Amen.

Day 26

Mary Magdalene and the Quest for Freedom

Now it came to pass, afterward, that He went through every city and village, preaching and bringing the glad tidings of the kingdom of God. And the twelve were with Him, and certain women who had been healed of evil spirits and infirmities—Mary called Magdalene, out of whom had come seven demons.

—Luke 8:1-2

God has made provision for our sin in Christ. So when we struggle to believe and obey, we should run to Him, not from Him—the opposite of our pattern, in contradiction to our feelings. Why? Because He already knows! See the gospel just keeps changing everything. The cross should continually testify to us that God fully knew we would need to be justified. Therefore, unconfessed sin is actually the foolish decision to run away from our healing and growth rather than toward it. We hang on to things we believe will satisfy us, thinking we need those more than what God offers to provide. But how can we rejoice in and worship the majesty of a loving and forgiving God if in practice we don't believe He loves and forgives, if in practice we don't believe the gospel? How can our churches rejoice and worship corporately when our collective energy is expended carrying around the saddle of unconfessed sin and shame? When people walk in honesty about their fears, shortcomings, and needs—not in thoughtless disobedience but in grace-based freedom and forgiveness—they reveal a deep understanding of the gospel. To confess our sins to one another is to violently pursue our own joy and the glory of God...and to exponentially increase our rejoicing and worship, both individually and corporately.

—Matt Chandler[1]

1 https://www.goodreads.com/quotes/search?commit=Search&page=3&q=freedom+in+chris t&utf8=□, accessed September 26, 2019

I absolutely love the story of Mary Magdalene. Though it has been twisted, misconstrued, and maligned down through the ages in one way or another (there are those who falsely claim that she was a prostitute, while others falsely claim that she was married to Jesus), her story as presented in the Bible is one of freedom, intrigue, service, discipleship, ministry, and partnering with her brothers in the Lord to fulfill His Great Commission.

We first read of Mary Magdalene in one of my favorite passages of Scripture, Luke 8:1-3. Not only was she one who accompanied Jesus wherever He went and ministered to Him from her own livelihood, but her story of coming to Christ in belief and salvation was quite the transformation story! She had been demon possessed by not one but seven demons, from which Christ delivered her. From that moment on, she was His faithful disciple and friend.

We see this illustrated most profoundly in the beautiful passage of Scripture describing Jesus' first moments as the resurrected Christ. John 20:1-18 says,

> Now the first day of the week Mary Magdalene went to the tomb early, while it was still dark, and saw that the stone had been taken away from the tomb. Then she ran and came to Simon Peter, and to the other disciple, whom Jesus loved, and said to them, "They have taken away the Lord out of the tomb, and we do not know where they have laid Him." Peter therefore went out, and the other disciple, and were going to the tomb. So they both ran together, and the other disciple outran Peter and came to the tomb first. And he, stooping down and looking in, saw the linen cloths lying there; yet he did not go in. Then Simon Peter came, following him, and went into the tomb; and he saw the linen cloths lying there, and the handkerchief that had been around His head, not lying with the linen cloths, but folded together in a place by itself. Then the other disciple, who came to the tomb first, went in also; and he saw and believed. For as yet they did not know the Scripture, that He must rise again from the dead. Then the disciples went away again to their own homes. But Mary stood outside by the tomb weeping, and as she wept she stooped down and looked into the tomb. And she saw two angels in white sitting, one at the head and the other at the feet, where the body of Jesus had lain. Then they said to her, "Woman, why are you weeping?" She

said to them, "Because they have taken away my Lord, and I do not know where they have laid Him." Now when she had said this, she turned around and saw Jesus standing there, and did not know that it was Jesus. Jesus said to her, "Woman, why are you weeping? Whom are you seeking?" She, supposing Him to be the gardener, said to Him, "Sir, if You have carried Him away, tell me where You have laid Him, and I will take Him away." Jesus said to her, "Mary!" She turned and said to Him, "Rabboni!" (which is to say, Teacher). Jesus said to her, "Do not cling to Me, for I have not yet ascended to My Father; but go to My brethren and say to them, 'I am ascending to My Father and your Father, and to My God and your God.'" Mary Magdalene came and told the disciples that she had seen the Lord, and that He had spoken these things to her.

I love this passage so much and for a multitude of reasons. Here was this woman whom Christ had rescued and freed from seven demons who were hell-bent on destroying her life. She had lost one of her dearest friends the day Jesus died, and now she is desperate to find His body when she discovers the tomb empty. We then see her overwhelming joy at the discovery that Jesus was now once again alive.

As if that isn't beautiful enough, then we see Jesus commission her—a woman—to be the first one to tell of the resurrection of Christ and to prophesy regarding His impending ascension back to the Father. In a time and place in which a woman's witness was not even worth half of a man's in a court of law, Jesus specifically chose Mary Magdalene to be the one to whom was entrusted the mission of proclaiming the resurrection of Christ. She became another in the line of the many female prophets God used down through history. That is quite striking if you think about it!

Not only did Mary Magdalene find freedom in Christ from seven demons, she also found freedom in Him from the patriarchal, misogynistic ways of her culture. Jesus ushered in a new way of viewing men and women—a way that was instituted way back in the garden but was lost at the onslaught of the fall. A way Paul describes so beautifully in Galatians (a book all about freedom). Galatians 3:28 says, "There is neither Jew nor Greek, there is neither slave nor free, there is neither male nor female; for you are all one in Christ Jesus."

Jesus loved and esteemed women in a time when they were daily downtrodden. He freed them from the bonds of slavery forced upon them by their culture and raised them up to partner with Him in the work of the ministry. That same beautiful freedom can also be yours today, friend, if you would but turn to Christ and take hold of it. After all, "Stand fast therefore in the liberty by which Christ has made us free, and do not be entangled again with a yoke of bondage" (Galatians 5:1).

Action Step:

Take some time to conduct your own study of women in the Bible whom God raised up, used, and freed from the lies and myths of their times. A great book to read on this topic, as mentioned in an earlier chapter, is *Vindicating the Vixens: Revisiting Sexualized, Vilified, and Marginalized Women of the Bible*, edited and compiled by Sandra Glahn.

Prayer:

Lord, thank You for the beautiful freedom that is mine in You. Thank You that I do not have to strive to prove myself, defend myself, or demand respect and position for myself. Rather, I can just rest in who You made me to be—an image bearer of You, equal to my brothers, and tasked just as they are with the Great Commission. Help me to be Your hands and feet, daily seeking to free other women by Your truth as You have freed me. In Jesus' name, Amen.

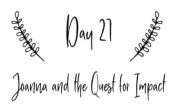

Day 21

Joanna and the Quest for Impact

Now it came to pass, afterward, that He went through every city and village, preaching and bringing the glad tidings of the kingdom of God. And the twelve were with Him, and certain women who had been healed of evil spirits and infirmities— Mary called Magdalene, out of whom had come seven demons, and Joanna the wife of Chuza, Herod's steward, and Susanna, and many others who provided for Him from their substance.

—Luke 8:1-3

Did you notice the part about women supporting men financially? The idea that men, and only men, must fully support financially the women in their families while the females do only domestic duties is a western middle-class construct that would never fly in the developing world today and certainly was not true in Jesus' time. Our Lord's practice of receiving the financial support of women suggests that doing so does not undermine manhood. And conversely, apparently a woman's femininity is not violated if she financially supports a man or men. In fact her doing so makes her a woman of hayil, a woman of valor, if her reason for doing so is because she wishes to bring glory to God.

—Sandra Glahn[1]

1 https://blogs.bible.org/engage/sandra_glahn/seriously_jesus_traveled_with_women, accessed September 19, 2019

I have shared in other books[2] I've written, as well as on my podcast[3] and other podcasts on which I have been a guest, that I went through a years-long season of legalism in my teen years. Part of the way in which this legalism manifested itself was in my view of what constituted truly biblical womanhood. I had a very narrow and confined view of God's design for womanhood—so narrow, in fact, that I believed if you were not either a stay-at-home daughter living under your father's roof until marriage or else a stay-at-home wife and mother following marriage, then there was no hope for you to be a "biblical woman."

What I didn't understand (besides the fact that none of that was actually biblical!) was that that particular view left out women who were single with no father in their lives, widowed, divorced, working, etc. In my narrow worldview at the time, in order to have a positive impact for the kingdom of God as a woman, you had to be waiting around to marry and be a mother—there were no other options.

And yet, this is not what we actually see in God's Word! What we see in the Word, for example, is what Luke shows us in the eighth chapter of his Gospel: that women were the ones who played a key role in sustaining, supporting, and encouraging Jesus' earthly ministry. Interestingly enough, as in the case of Joanna, at least some of these women were married and presumably had children at home.

Why is this interesting? Because in the kind of ultra-conservative construct from which I operated for so many years, to do what Joanna did (being a wife and yet not staying at home but rather traveling with and supporting Jesus) would have been to sin against God's design for her as a woman.

This is not at all what we see portrayed in this passage, however. Instead, we see Luke intentionally point out and praise these women for the key role of impact they played in advancing and making possible Christ's day-in and day-out ministry. They were His comrades and partners in ministry, they supported Him financially, and they encouraged Him. They made quite an impact to be sure!

Perhaps you have been in a season of striving lately. You have been striving to prove yourself, to defend your gender, to shout, "I am woman, hear me roar!" to those who think that you are deprived of the opportunity to make a difference in this world because of your womanhood. Maybe you have been striving to justify yourself, to pile so much on your plate in the hope of having an impact in some tangible way. My friend, this Lenten season, cease your striving.

---

2 https://www.hargraveshomeandhearth.com/e-book/
3 https://www.hargraveshomeandhearth.com/podcast

Instead, take heart! Rejoice in who God made you to be as a woman! Delight in the example of women like Joanna, Huldah, and others who impacted God's kingdom for eternity. You can do the same! Just remain in step with the Holy Spirit and allow Him to lead you every step of the way. He will grow you, sanctify you, and equip you to be on mission and to live a life of kingdom impact in big ways and in small ways every day of your life. God created you as a woman for a purpose. Now go out there and live it out!

Action Step:

Spend some time in prayer, asking the Lord to show you what He would have you do in this season to impact His kingdom for eternity. And, if you haven't already, order yourself a copy of *Vindicating the Vixens* (edited and compiled by Sandra Glahn, whom I quoted above) and move it to the top of your list of books to read. You will be glad you did!

Prayer:

Lord, thank You for the freedom I am finding in You. Thank You for the realization that I can and should live a life of impact for Your kingdom. Help me to walk in that freedom, while at the same time remaining in tune to Your Spirit so that I won't hustle, strive, or live a life of overwhelm. Instead, help me to be still and know that You are God, even as I seek to leave behind a legacy of impact. Help me to strike that balance. In Jesus' name, Amen.

Day 28

Mary and the Quest for Relationship

Now it happened as they went that He entered a certain village; and a certain woman named Martha welcomed Him into her house. And she had a sister called Mary, who also sat at Jesus' feet and heard His word. But Martha was distracted with much serving, and she approached Him and said, "Lord, do You not care that my sister has left me to serve alone? Therefore tell her to help me." And Jesus answered and said to her, "Martha, Martha, you are worried and troubled about many things. But one thing is needed, and Mary has chosen that good part, which will not be taken away from her."

—Luke 10:38-42

We're here to be worshipers first and workers only second. We take a convert and immediately make a worker out of him. God never meant it to be so. God meant that a convert should learn to be a worshiper, and after that he can learn to be a worker... The work done by a worshiper will have eternity in it.

—A.W. Tozer[1]

Ahhh, the biblical story of Mary and Martha. It is a story with which many of us are familiar—one which tends to spark feelings of frustration and cause shouts of "That's not fair!" to rise from the hearts of tired, overworked, weary women everywhere. I believe we do ourselves a great disservice, however, when we stop there, lick our

---

1 http://christian-quotes.ochristian.com/christian-quotes_ochristian.cgi?query=learn&action=Search&x=0&y=0, accessed September 16, 2019

proverbial wounds, and do not take the time to stop and ponder what the Lord could be trying to teach us through this narrative. I believe this is a very applicable, relevant story from which we women can actually glean some much needed wisdom, insight, relief, and encouragement that will serve to bolster us in our walks as busy women. The story is a short, though profoundly life-changing, one found in the Gospel of Luke. We'll look at it from Mary's point of view today and then turn our attention to Martha tomorrow.

I already know what you are likely thinking right now! *Only one thing is needed?? **Mary** chose the good part? Are you sure, Lord? I thought we were supposed to serve others! I thought we were supposed to take care of our homes, practice hospitality, and care for our families? What about that? What about my lengthy to-do list??* I hear you, friend! I understand what it is to feel overwhelmed, for it to seem like you have a million and one important tasks weighing on you, and it is all you can do to just get through the day. But may I share a little something with you, dear reader? I believe it is precisely because the Lord knows these feelings that rage in the hearts of us women, the struggles we go through, and the expectations we heap upon ourselves, that He chose to include such an admonition as this in His Word in the first place.

The Lord knows we as women are "worried and troubled about many things." He was the One who fashioned and designed us, making us to be caregivers, helpers, and nurturers in this life. He knows well all that goes along with that—the encouraging and helping of husbands, the discipling and training of children day in and day out, the running of the home, and the list goes on.

Our God is a loving, compassionate, merciful, tender Father who delights in strengthening, helping, bolstering, encouraging, and serving us, His precious daughters. The key here is this: He understands better than anyone that true rest and needed refreshment for the race set before us come not in the marking off of tasks on the to-do list (though we do find enjoyment in that sometimes), but rather in the moments spent with our Lord, learning from Him, reading His Word, and communing with Him in prayer.

Now, before the exhausted mama of littles gets all up in arms at what I am saying, let me set your heart at ease! Mama, this is not about Pharisaical legalism or a list of rules which includes an expectation that you should get up at 4am every morning, spend an hour in Bible study, then an hour in prayer, and, finally, an hour in Scripture memorization, all before those kiddos of yours get up. Nor am I advocating the practice of allowing your little ones to veg out in front of the TV so that you can have four hours of inductive Bible study on a regular basis. But it is about realizing that we do tend to make time for what is truly important to us, and that whether or not we are in the Word has a far greater impact on how the rest of our day goes than we oftentimes realize. And, if we want to do this whole Christian woman, wife, and mama thing well, we are going to have to tap into the strength and inspiration of God. It is the only way! So, what can today's Christian woman learn from the biblical narrative of Mary and Martha? Well, let's dive right in and see, again focusing on Mary's perspective first.

In this passage, Jesus says one thing is important: sitting at His feet. Why? Because it is this practice which reminds us daily of who we are in Christ. It is a wonderful antidote against striving to prove ourselves, impress the Lord or others, or work ourselves to the bone as did Martha, because we think we have to or that God would love us more if we did. What we have to remember is that the Lord does not need our work, our striving, or our to-do lists. He wants our hearts.

A friend shared with me the following quote a while back, and it has remained with me ever since:

> We are often eager to listen to the voices that say, "Prove yourself, do something important, succeed, achieve!" rather than God's voice, which whispers, "Rest in Me; I am your Shepherd. You don't have to prove anything. You are not an employee. You are My child." Our activity is not synonymous with our identity."[2]

You are not God's employee, dear sister! You are His precious, beloved, bought-with-a-price child. You are His creation and His daughter and one who has the imputed righteousness of Christ fully clothing you every moment of every day!

This Lenten season and on into every other day of your life, do not strive after endless to-do lists. (For they really are endless, as there is always something we women feel like needs done, and we think we always have to be the ones to do it.) Do not worry and fret that you are not doing "enough." Do not flit around like Martha, trying to make everything in life just perfect for your family, friends, guests, and others. You will likely overwhelm yourself, losing sight of the whole purpose behind what you are doing and coming to disdain it and allowing a root of bitterness to grow in your heart. Do not burn out in your life's work because you have been so focused on being God's

---

2 From the book *Replenish* by Lance Witt.

employee that you forget that "It is finished"—that Christ performed everything necessary through both His perfect life and His death on the cross to redeem you, justify you, sanctify you, and one day glorify you (Romans 8:29-30).

Everything has been done, and if you have trusted fully in Christ's work on your behalf, He sees you as perfect. Nothing you can do will ever make Him love you more or less or cause Him to be more impressed with you or less impressed with you. So, stop striving, friend.

This isn't to say that you throw off doing any housework and become a lazy bum—we are going to look at things from Martha's perspective tomorrow, after all! However, being a "Martha" and serving begrudgingly does no one any good. Constantly trying to cross things off our to-do list to the detriment of spending time with God is not a right ordering of priorities. The only way to combat these issues is by being more like Mary, placing a high priority on just sitting at Jesus' feet and realizing that, though we women may sometimes feel guilty about taking the time to do so and feel as if there are other pressing things to do instead, this practice of spending time with Jesus, sharing our hearts with Him as with a dear friend, and learning from Him is the only way to arm ourselves for the battles ahead. It is crucially important. It is not something to take or leave, to do when we feel like it, etc.

Jesus likens God's Word to daily nourishment. We would not just eat physical food here or there until we discover we are suddenly starving and close to death. No, we eat every day in order to fuel our bodies. So, too, must we be at the feet of Jesus and in His Word on a regular basis in order to fuel our souls and spirits. What better time to begin than right now during Lent?

Action Step:

Take a moment to just sit and meditate on the quote shared above that my friend shared with me. Mull its truth over and over in your mind, allowing it to change and reframe how you view your identity.

Prayer:

Lord, thank You for this picture in the book of Luke of an endearing, close, intimate friendship with You. Thank You that in a patriarchal culture wherein women were not allowed to learn at the feet of a teacher alongside the men, that You instead welcomed Mary there, told her that was where she belonged, and rebuked anyone that would tell her otherwise. Help me to carry this picture in my heart throughout my days, allowing it to impact the way I view myself and my relationship with You. May it deepen my desire to be in daily close relationship with You in the first place. In Jesus' name, Amen.

Day 29

Martha and the Quest for Help

Now it happened as they went that He entered a certain village; and a certain woman named Martha welcomed Him into her house. And she had a sister called Mary, who also sat at Jesus' feet and heard His word. But Martha was distracted with much serving, and she approached Him and said, "Lord, do You not care that my sister has left me to serve alone? Therefore tell her to help me." And Jesus answered and said to her, "Martha, Martha, you are worried and troubled about many things. But one thing is needed, and Mary has chosen that good part, which will not be taken away from her."

—Luke 10:38-42

The local church is espoused to Christ, but there is always the danger of that love growing cold. Like Martha, we can be so busy working for Christ that we have no time to love Him. Christ is more concerned about what we do with Him than for Him. Labor is no substitute for love. To the public, the Ephesian church was successful; to Christ, it had fallen.

—Warren Wiersbe[1]

At first glance, it would seem, perhaps, that Jesus is overly exaggerating or maybe even a little wrong when He says to Martha that only one thing is needed, and that Mary has chosen that better part. After all, does not Proverbs 31:10-31 go on and on about all that the godly wife and mother was doing in and around her home? Doesn't it speak of her spinning thread, making clothing, looking well to the

1 http://christian-quotes.ochristian.com/christian-quotes_ochristian.cgi?query=martha&action=Search&x=0&y=0, accessed September 16, 2019

ways of her household, conducting business, traveling far and wide to gather the best food possible for her family, serving the poor and needy, and making meals? Judging from the tasks alone, that sounds a lot like Martha.

Furthermore, we might be wondering how this fits with what we read in Titus 2. Does it not say that we, as women, are to be busy at home so that the Word of God is not blasphemed? Sounds pretty crucial to me! Aren't we as women to be, as is stated in Proverbs 14:1, wise and build our homes rather than foolishly tear them down with our own hands? But consider with me this truth for a moment: We cannot conduct the roles of wife, mother, and homemaker well unless we are regularly tapping into the Lord, His truth, and His strength. We cannot conduct our other roles well as women if we do not first begin at the beginning and build a firm foundation of relationship.

For example, not only did the Proverbs 31 woman fill her time with making meals and sewing tapestry, but we also see that she feared God (vs. 30) and opened her mouth with wisdom (vs.26)—feats which would have been impossible had she not first been a student of the Word, seeking and acquiring the wisdom of God, since true wisdom comes only from the Lord (Prov. 1:7; 2:6; 15:33). Likewise, reading further into Titus 2:4-5, we see that women are not merely to be homemakers but also loving, good, chaste, and discreet—characteristics which mirror the fruits of the Spirit (Gal. 5:22-23) and are only cultivated through the work of God in our hearts and lives and through our daily pursuit of Him.

The work of the home is indeed to be one of our primary priorities as women, and the nurture and care of our families are some of our most important roles. But God is to be of first priority in our lives, and it is only by learning from and about Him and His example that we are equipped for the myriad important daily tasks set before us.

So, why does Jesus say but one thing is needed? Because as we learned yesterday, that one thing—being at the feet of Jesus to listen to and learn from Him—carries out into all other areas of life, touching and affecting each and every one. As a friend made the point to me a while back, "Perhaps Martha would have had the strength, grace, and servant's heart required for her tasks if she had first met with Jesus and spent time at His feet."

Oftentimes we busy women allow our daily quiet times to be the first thing to go when life speeds up, and we begin to feel weighed down by it all. But that is the biggest mistake we can make in those moments. It is like cutting ourselves off from an IV that is infusing life-giving medicine into our bodies. It zaps us of the strength, vision, endurance, love, purpose, joy, stamina, and grace required for this marathon called life. We need that time in the Word!

Sadly, however, those moments with the Lord are the first and easiest to see go because, after all, no one will notice the difference, right? My family will definitely notice if there is no food on the table or if the laundry remains piled on the floor or if they step foot into that bathtub that hasn't seen a good cleaning in far too long. But what if I don't read my Bible today or even this week? How would they even know? Trust me—they will feel the difference.

The atmosphere of our homes will undoubtedly feel different. They will notice that we are more stressed, more cranky and irritable, and more likely to grow frustrated, exhausted, or discouraged. I know I, for one, notice a big difference in my entire outlook on the rest of my day if I do not have my daily quiet time first thing in the morning after my husband leaves for work and before my kids get up. I am more easily frustrated or irritable, and even my energy and exuberance for the day's tasks can more easily wane. When I start my day in God's Word, however, I am uplifted and better equipped and prepared for whatever lies ahead. Second Timothy 3:16-17 speaks to this phenomenon:

> All Scripture is given by inspiration of God, and is profitable for doctrine, for reproof, for correction, for instruction in righteousness, that the man of God may be complete, thoroughly equipped for every good work.

Time in the Word is not something to take off the to-do list when the days get hurried and harried. Focusing on our to-do lists and having it be our mission to daily complete as many of the tasks on them as possible is not what will lead us and our loved ones closer to Christ. Yes, homemaking tasks are important, but I believe we would all agree that souls are far more so. Regular time in the Word is crucial, for we cannot pass on what we do not have. It isn't that work and homemaking are unimportant tasks. It is that we have to have the truth and encouragement of the Word in our hearts in order for it to equip us for those important tasks at hand.

Action Step:

Assess your current typical to-do list and ask yourself what you can remove from that list, replacing that less important task with the all-important practice of communing with the Lord through His Word and prayer. Make this a daily habit throughout the rest of the Lenten season and see what a difference it makes.

Prayer:

Lord, I know the work to which You have called me is important. And I thank You for it. My days are not truly mundane or purposeless. But I also know that I tend to relegate the most important thing—time spent with You—to the back burner. Help me to change that, Lord. Give me the strength to do what I know is most important, not just those tasks from which I more readily see a return on investment right away. Help me to live with an eternal perspective. Thank You for the gift that is Your Word. In Jesus' name, Amen.

Day 30

Tabitha and the Quest for Healing

At Joppa there was a certain disciple named Tabitha, which is translated Dorcas. This woman was full of good works and charitable deeds which she did. But it happened in those days that she became sick and died. When they had washed her, they laid her in an upper room. And since Lydda was near Joppa, and the disciples had heard that Peter was there, they sent two men to him, imploring him not to delay in coming to them. Then Peter arose and went with them. When he had come, they brought him to the upper room. And all the widows stood by him weeping, showing the tunics and garments which Dorcas had made while she was with them. But Peter put them all out, and knelt down and prayed. And turning to the body he said, "Tabitha, arise." And she opened her eyes, and when she saw Peter she sat up. Then he gave her his hand and lifted her up; and when he had called the saints and widows, he presented her alive. And it became known throughout all Joppa, and many believed on the Lord.

—Acts 9:36-42

Come, and see the victories of the cross. Christ's wounds are thy healings, His agonies thy repose, His conflicts thy conquests, His groans thy songs, His pains thine ease, His shame thy glory, His death thy life, His sufferings thy salvation.

—Matthew Henry[1]

---

1 https://www.christianquotes.info/quotes-by-topic/quotes-about-the-cross/

Many lies and misconceptions get thrown around in the church today surrounding the topic of healing. There are those who will say the miracles of healing have completely ceased, while others say that God wants all believers to be healthy, wealthy, and prosperous at all times. There are those "evangelists" who will charge you for a healing, and others who say you just have to suffer through whatever comes your way, and to seek healing and restoration is asking too much. They are the same ones who are against women having epidurals—not because they think there are benefits to natural childbirth, but they think that since pain in childbirth is a result of the fall, we are required to suffer through it.

I must say I do love the story of Tabitha (or Dorcas) found in Acts 9. This was a woman who loved God and loved others so much so that her very reputation itself was that she was "full of good works and charitable deeds which she did." These were not things she did sparingly; her life was full of them. You can imagine the grief, then, felt by the whole town when they heard she had passed.

Tabitha's story certainly isn't the story of everyone who passes away, but it is an amazing story showcasing the power of God and the part that miracles have played in His plan down through the ages. What is hard, though, is when that story is not your own or the one of someone close to you. When your beloved grandfather goes into cardiac arrest and the doctors aren't able to bring him back. When you watch your sister-in-law lose her baby just an hour after birth. When someone else you know has cancer, and it's up in the air as to whether or not it will go into remission, let alone stay in remission. Life is hard, and situations such as these are far too common for many of us. Chances are, we have all known someone who has died of cancer no matter what the doctors, pastor, and praying Christian friends tried to do.

The answer in times like that, however, is not to give up on one's faith. It isn't to throw in the towel and say God really fell asleep at the wheel that time. It isn't to spout off nonsense about that person not having had enough faith or else they would be well. Instead, it is time to look to the future joy and hope we have awaiting us in heaven. Revelation 21:4 reminds us of this beautiful time we have awaiting us, a promised time that we will enjoy no matter what befalls us in this life: "And God will wipe away every tear from their eyes; there shall be no more death, nor sorrow, nor crying. There shall be no more pain, for the former things have passed away."

God is not a cosmic killjoy or a sadistic ruler bent on sending destruction and pain our way. But death and loss and pain and destruction are results of the choices we have made on our own to go against God's perfect ways for us. As a result, we battle sicknesses, lose loved ones, and walk through life with holes in our hearts as a result. And while God does promise that good will come out of each and every not-so-good thing we face in this life, sometimes the fulfillment of that promise feels a long way off. Sometimes God does heal people in this life from their infirmities, but sometimes He doesn't. And we have to be able to look beyond the pain of the here and now and on into the joy that is awaiting us for eternity.

I know that the temptation is to strive to find answers and seek healings and make restoration happen if something is broken and unhealthy in your life. While there is nothing necessarily wrong with seeking to find answers and attain solutions, this Lenten season may we cease our constant striving and rest in the arms of Jesus, the One Who loves us more than anyone else ever could and has a reason for everything He does.

Look to Him this season, friend, knowing that He has everything under control. And even if you do not acquire the healing you seek in the transient here and now, it will be yours in the eternal kingdom. How much more valuable that truly is!

Action Step:

Pour out your concerns and desires to the Lord. Make a list of the loved ones you know who are currently battling one disease or another, or those who have a spiritual, emotional, or mental issue for which they need healing. Seek to be an aid to them in any way you can, while ultimately keeping your eyes fixed on God's big-picture perspective and His loving character that determines all He does.

Prayer:

Lord, it hurts when we need healing, and it's nowhere to be found. It shakes our faith and pains our hearts. But, Lord, we want to trust in You even as we seek a resolution. Help me to trust in You more, to rest in Your ways and Your love, knowing that it is Your love that determines all you do in my life. In Jesus' name, Amen.

Day 31

Lydia and the Quest for Hospitality

Therefore, sailing from Troas, we ran a straight course to Samothrace, and the next day came to Neapolis, and from there to Philippi, which is the foremost city of that part of Macedonia, a colony. And we were staying in that city for some days. And on the Sabbath day we went out of the city to the riverside, where prayer was customarily made; and we sat down and spoke to the women who met there. Now a certain woman named Lydia heard us. She was a seller of purple from the city of Thyatira, who worshiped God. The Lord opened her heart to heed the things spoken by Paul. And when she and her household were baptized, she begged us, saying, "If you have judged me to be faithful to the Lord, come to my house and stay." So she persuaded us.

—Acts 16:11-15

The deep-seated worrying, the excuses, and the overthinking of a simple invitation should be warning signs, telling us we're confusing social entertaining with hospitality. When we use our lives exactly as they are, desiring only to create a sacred space for our guests, mixing it with the countercultural truth of loving Jesus and loving others, we turn entertaining upside down, and it becomes radical hospitality.

—Jen Schmidt[1]

---

1 https://www.goodreads.com/quotes/search?utf8=□&q=jen+schmidt&commit=Search, accessed September 30, 2019

The ministry of hospitality is not dependent on a particular personality trait. It does not stem from whether one is an introvert or extravert, an enneagram 7 or an enneagram 1. Hospitality is also not just for those who are gifted in the art of home decor, creative design ideas, or gourmet cooking on a budget. Instead, the ministry of hospitality, even just the desire itself to extend hospitality to others, stems first and foremost from an acknowledgement of what God has done in our lives.

We see this exemplified so beautifully in the story of Lydia. She was a creative businesswoman and most likely a seamstress, who was regularly given to the worship of God and prayer. When she, through Paul, became exposed to further truth about the God she worshiped, her desire was to be baptized. Her immediate next response was this: "If you have judged me to be faithful to the Lord, come to my house and stay." Immediately following God's work in her heart and her subsequent baptism, her response is that she yearned to extend hospitality to this man who has spoken biblical truth to her and ministered to her.

What Lydia does in this passage is not begrudgingly offer an invitation to her home because she feels as if she has to or merely believes it is the right thing to do—a practice with which Christians are tasked. No, it's much more than that. She literally begs them to come to her home and allow her to care for them. That, friends, is how we ought to be when considering the topic of extending hospitality to someone.

Hospitality is not about striving for perfection, entertaining, impressing people, or having the most spotless home, tastiest food, and in-vogue decor. It is about loving God and loving others. It is about so delighting in, resting in, and flourishing in God's love for you that you can't help but pour that love back out on others. It's about being so grateful for God's love, mercy, and grace that you can't wait to extend that same love, mercy, and grace to everyone you know to whom you might could open your door.

Truly, hospitality is an outpouring to others of what God has given to you. When you keep that in mind, it becomes so much easier to cease the striving, the stress, and the sense of overwhelm at the thought of having people into your home. Because it isn't about you anymore. It's about God's goodness and the well-being of those who enter your home. With that proper perspective in place, it won't matter if what you serve is pizza on paper plates—your guests would probably prefer that anyway! It won't matter if your sink is full of dishes and there are crumbs on your floor—your guests will probably feel much more at home!

It isn't that we shouldn't seek to care well for our homes and offer our guests the best. But it is that we are ready and willing, from a heart of love rather than performance and pride, to throw open our doors to guests no matter when it is and what the state of our homes may be in that moment. After all, the ministry of hospitality is just that—a ministry!

Action Step:

Look at your calendar and choose a day when you could have someone over for dinner or for just coffee and a chat. Extend the invitation.

Prayer:

Lord, thank You for the ministry of hospitality You have entrusted to me as a believer. Too often I get all caught up in what my home looks like or how good the food is, when instead I should just be focusing on how I can pour out the love on others that You have so graciously and generously poured out on me. Help me to take this ministry seriously—not from a place of striving, but rather from a place of it being the natural outpouring of my relationship with You. In Jesus' name, Amen.

Day 32

Priscilla and the Quest for Boldness

This man had been instructed in the way of the Lord; and being fervent in spirit, he spoke and taught accurately the things of the Lord, though he knew only the baptism of John. So he began to speak boldly in the synagogue. When Aquila and Priscilla heard him, they took him aside and explained to him the way of God more accurately. And when he desired to cross to Achaia, the brethren wrote, exhorting the disciples to receive him; and when he arrived, he greatly helped those who had believed through grace.

—Acts 18:25-27

There's a difference between knowing God and knowing about God. When you truly know God, you have energy to serve him, boldness to share him, and contentment in him.

—J.I. Packer[1]

Priscilla is such a wonderful example for women in the church.[2] We are first introduced to her in Acts 18:2, when Luke tells us that she and her husband, Aquila, were from Italy. Paul stayed with them for a time, ministering to others alongside them and also working in their tent-making business. In verse 24 we read that a fellow minister of the Lord, Apollos, came to Ephesus and began to preach in the

---

1 http://christian-quotes.ochristian.com/christian-quotes_ochristian.cgi?query=bold&action=Search&x=0&y=0, accessed September 16, 2019

2 A portion of this section is based on a blog post I wrote - https://www.angelpenn.com/priscilla-taught-me/, accessed September 16, 2019

synagogue. Though much of what he was teaching was correct, and he was a fervent, eloquent man, he nevertheless was proclaiming some falsehoods in his gospel presentations. In verse 26 Priscilla arrives on the scene again and we read this:

> When Aquila and Priscilla heard him (Apollos), they took him aside and explained to him the way of God more accurately.

Did you catch that? Both Aquila and Priscilla took this preacher and teacher of God aside and taught him the full truth of God's Word and the gospel. This is a crystal clear case of a woman teaching God's truth to a man, and Paul (the same one who penned 1 Timothy 2 and 1 Corinthians 14) never once rebuked her for it! In fact, he seems to have thought very highly of both her and her husband, choosing to work and minister closely alongside them and commending them and their work to others. Paul even refers to them in Romans 16:3 as being his "fellow workers in Christ Jesus."

I went through a long season of legalism, beginning in my mid-teens and continuing on a bit into my early twenties, when it came to what I believed biblical womanhood to be. It has been quite a journey in recent years of the Lord opening my eyes to the full-orbed richness of His design for women. As I have intently studied the Word of God in general, and certain women in the Word in particular, in order to form my current understanding of what it means to be a Christian woman, one of the women that has stood out to me the most is Priscilla. Her example has been used by God to encourage, inspire, and equip me in my walk as a biblical woman of influence myself.

One of the things I am learning from Priscilla is that I need to be willing to proclaim the Word. I need to, as 2 Timothy 4:2 says, "Preach the word! Be ready in season and out of season. Convince, rebuke, exhort, with all longsuffering and teaching." Priscilla, when faced with error and unsound doctrine, was ready and able to address and refute it with the truths of God. If we want to be biblical women of influence, we have to be willing to do so, too. And what equips us to be able to do that? Being in the Word and knowing the Word.

Even more than that, however, I also have to understand my identity as a minister of the gospel. Priscilla's example teaches me that I, as a Christian, am called to be a minister of the gospel. In Romans 16:3, Paul refers to Priscilla and Aquila in this way: "Greet Priscilla and Aquila, my fellow workers in Christ Jesus." I am called to be a co-laborer in the truth alongside my brothers and sisters in Christ and can teach both men and women the truths of God's Word. In order to be a true biblical woman of influence as was Priscilla, I need to be viewing every day of my life (and every aspect of my every day) as being a part of the Great Commission work to which I have been called. Whether I am sweeping the floor, cleaning the tub, schooling little ones, making meals, writing books, recording podcasts, speaking to women, extending hospitality, going to the grocery store, taking a walk in my neighborhood, texting a friend, or reading to my children, I need to be doing all of that with the understanding that not one single aspect of that work is mundane. Rather, it can all be done to the glory of God and for the advancement of His glorious kingdom.

We can know all these truths and yet still not fully become biblical women of influence like Priscilla, as there was something else she was known for: her boldness. Now, this can seem incredibly discouraging and like it's just one more thing for which you have to strive if you are of the mindset that you have to grow, change, and sanctify yourself. But the good news is you don't have to do any of that! All you have to do is walk by the Spirit (see Galatians 5:16-18).[3]

As you intentionally remain in God's Word, in prayer, and in godly Christian community, you will find it becomes second nature to be in step with the Holy Spirit, following His guidance and direction in your life. And that, my friend, will naturally lead to increased boldness in your proclamation of His truth. Don't strive, friend. Just walk...by the Spirit!

Action Step:

Read Galatians 5 and discover how the fruits of the Spirit are cultivated in your life. Read John 15 and see what Christ has to say about abiding in Him. Meditate on the truths of these two chapters and ask yourself what part Paul's and Jesus' teachings play in your ability to grow in boldness.

---

3 For more on this topic, check out the magazine I co-founded, Spirit-Filled Woman Magazine, as well as our brand new book on what it means to walk by the Spirit at www.spiritfilledwoman-mag.com/shop

Prayer:

Lord, thank You that it isn't just during this Lenten season that I don't have to strive, but that You actually call me to cease from striving every day of the year. What a gift it is to know that I do not have to force or make myself to be bold, and that I don't have to stress over growing in boldness. Instead, I can just walk in step with You and watch as You work in my heart and life. Thank You for this grace. In Jesus' name, Amen.

Day 33

Lois and Eunice and the Quest for a Godly Legacy

I thank God, whom I serve with a pure conscience, as my forefathers did, as without ceasing I remember you in my prayers night and day, greatly desiring to see you, being mindful of your tears, that I may be filled with joy, when I call to remembrance the genuine faith that is in you, which dwelt first in your grandmother Lois and your mother Eunice, and I am persuaded is in you also..... But you must continue in the things which you have learned and been assured of, knowing from whom you have learned them, and that from childhood you have known the Holy Scriptures, which are able to make you wise for salvation through faith which is in Christ Jesus.

—2 Timothy 1:3-5; 3:14-15

[A woman's] education should be as varied and perfect as possible. If for no other reason to enable her properly to educate and rear her own children. Whatever grand truths are planted in the mother's mind may take root in the next generation, and there grow, blossom, and shed their perfume on the world. The child receives the mother's very thought by intuition. If the mother's mind is weak and narrow in its range, the child is affected by this fact long before it finds meaning in the mother's words. But if the mother's mind is cultured and refined by study until her thoughts are grand and far-reaching, the child's soul will grow and expand under the mesmeric influence of these thoughts, as the plant grows under the influence of the sun.

—Karen Andreola[1]

1 https://www.goodreads.com/quotes/search?utf8=✓&q=mother%27s+influence&commit=Search, accessed September 28, 2019

Parenting may well be the hardest task some of us ever put our hands to. Stewarding well the eternal souls entrusted to our care is no small matter—a fact of which many of us are well aware and which leaves us fretting on at least a semi-regular basis. We agonize over feeding methods and schedules when our children are babies, and we research sleep training, proper car seat practices, and best health choices for the well-being of their immune systems. Then, as our children get older, we fret over how best to educate them—whether to do it ourselves or choose one of the many public or private school options. Then, if we choose to homeschool, we spend hours upon hours trying to find the "perfect" homeschooling method or curriculum. All along the way, we compare, compete with, or copy other moms.

In addition to all the physical and everyday worries we have as moms, there are spiritual worries we have as well: How do we raise kids who will love and choose to follow Christ? How will we develop in our kids a love for the Word and prayer, and a desire to be daily connected to both? How can we ensure that our kids will be joining us in Heaven one day?

Well, the truth of the matter is we can't. We can't ensure that any of that will happen, and on our own we cannot develop in our kids a love for God. In fact, we were never meant to. And yet, as moms we spend so much of our time stressing and striving, attempting to dot every "i" and cross every "t." But, friend, that life of striving was never what God intended for us! It is good and appropriate for us to desire to live and mother in such a way that we would leave behind a godly legacy one day. But striving for it and believing ourselves to be the Holy Spirit is not what will get us there. That will only serve to steal the joy we could otherwise have if we would sit back a bit and let God be God.

We all know that we cannot make another person say, think, or do the things we want.[2] We know we can't force another adult into being the kind of person we think they should be. Yet that is precisely what we end up doing with our children. We somehow think that what is true for adults simply can't be true for our children. We believe that if we only use the right training method, discipline consistently and in the manner which best suits each particular child, read the Bible and

---

2 A portion of this section originally appeared in Rebekah Hargraves, *Lies Moms Believe (And How the Gospel Refutes Them)* (Rebekah Hargraves: 2018)

pray with them daily, follow all the rules pertaining to baby care, tend to toddler tantrums the way in which the books tell us, implement the perfect homeschool curriculum, give our children the best devotional books available, always take them to church, and surround them with good, Christian friends, then all will be well. And if it isn't, then clearly there was some box left unchecked, some book that was not read, or some chore chart that was not implemented, and it is all our fault.

This, however, is not God's point of view. This kind of mindset of striving and self-help actually takes God out of the equation entirely. Oh, He's factored in somewhere in the sense that we are placing value on taking our children to church, surrounding them with good company, and encouraging them to read a daily devotional. But He is left out of the equation in the sense that we are acting as if we don't truly need Him. As long as we dot all our "i's" and cross all our "t's," we have it all covered, are guaranteed to produce perfect little Christians, and don't really need God's involvement, thank you very much.

With a viewpoint such as this, there is no parenting by faith, there is no seeking God for help and wisdom, there is no praying for the Lord to touch the hearts of our children. There is simply a trusting in our own efforts. There is simply a belief that if I am a good mom, my kids will be good. If my kids are bad, then that must mean I am a bad mom. But in all our striving, there is an important passage to sit back and remember:

> Who then is Paul, and who is Apollos, but ministers through whom you believed, as the Lord gave to each one? I planted, Apollos watered, but God gave the increase. So then neither he who plants is anything, nor he who waters, but God who gives the increase.

> —1 Corinthians 3:5-7

As you can see, the responsibility for the results of our parenting efforts lies solely on the Lord. We cannot, therefore, believe ourselves to be "bad moms" if our children go astray. We cannot believe the lie that our success is solely dependent upon what we do or don't do. We certainly have a role and responsibility to play, just as did Paul and Apollos. We train our children up in the way they should go, raise them in the nurture and admonition of the Lord, and we speak of the Word to them as we lie down, as we rise up, and as we go about our days together. But the lasting results, the heart change, and the legacy is something the Holy Spirit must see to.

This is not to say that we as mothers (or grandmothers!) do not have a powerful influence. We absolutely do! We see Paul praise both Lois and Eunice for the hugely important part they played in young Timothy's life and his ability to know and love the Lord and His Word. But this truth is a far cry from the kind of enslaving idea that it all depends on us. Because truly it doesn't.

Action Step:

Commit your way to the Lord and take some time to read Psalm 37 if you haven't in a while. Surrender your mothering and your children to Him, asking Him to work in your children and through your parenting efforts. Lay the striving down at His feet and trust in His plan for your children.

Prayer:

Lord, thank You that the eternal well-being of my children is not ultimately dependent upon me. It's such a relief to know that I can cease my striving in this area and let go of the feeling that I have to get my act together in order to ensure success and a godly legacy. Thank You for the role You have given to me, and help me to live it out well. But also please help me to rest in the glorious truth that I am not the Holy Spirit and do not have to act like it. In Jesus' name, Amen.

Part 2

The Path to the Cross

Day 34

Jesus' Triumphal Entry and The Need for a Messiah

The next day a great multitude that had come to the feast, when they heard that Jesus was coming to Jerusalem, took branches of palm trees and went out to meet Him, and cried out: "Hosanna! Blessed is He who comes in the name of the Lord! The King of Israel!" Then Jesus, when He had found a young donkey, sat on it; as it is written: "Fear not, daughter of Zion; behold, your King is coming, sitting on a donkey's colt." His disciples did not understand these things at first; but when Jesus was glorified, then they remembered that these things were written about Him and that they had done these things to Him. Therefore the people, who were with Him when He called Lazarus out of his tomb and raised him from the dead, bore witness. For this reason the people also met Him, because they heard that He had done this sign.

—John 12:12-18

For much of Jesus' ministry He urged people to be quiet about who He was. When He healed He told people not to say anything, when He confronted demons who recognized Him as the Son of God He told them to shut up. That's because it wasn't time for Him to declare Himself as the Messiah. On Palm Sunday the time had come.

—Tom Fuller[1]

---

1 https://www.sermoncentral.com/pastors-preaching-articles/sermoncentral-21-palm-sunday-quotes-that-will-preach-3154, accessed October 2, 2019

During our final week of study together (this final week of Lent), we will be taking a look at each of the days of what has become known as "Holy Week," the week between Palm Sunday, which we read about above, and Resurrection Sunday, when we celebrate Easter.

To me, Palm Sunday is a rather bittersweet part of this week. On the one hand, it is a joy to see Jesus receive the laud and honor He so greatly deserved. And yet, it is hard to read about, knowing full well that those very same people who are praising Him are about to cry out, "Crucify Him!" in but a few short days. How fickle is the honor of fallen human beings.

Just the day before the triumphal entry, we see again this separation between those who were truly Jesus' friends and those who wanted to see Him killed. John 12:1-3 says,

> Then, six days before the Passover, Jesus came to Bethany, where Lazarus was who had been dead, whom He had raised from the dead. There they made Him a supper; and Martha served, but Lazarus was one of those who sat at the table with Him. Then Mary took a pound of very costly oil of spikenard, anointed the feet of Jesus, and wiped His feet with her hair. And the house was filled with the fragrance of the oil.

Contrast that with John 12:9-11:

> Now a great many of the Jews knew that He was there; and they came, not for Jesus' sake only, but that they might also see Lazarus, whom He had raised from the dead. But the chief priests plotted to put Lazarus to death also, because on account of him many of the Jews went away and believed in Jesus.

The chief priests were so vicious that not only did they want to kill Jesus, they wanted to kill Lazarus, too! Though raising Lazarus from the dead was all Jesus' doing, and Lazarus had nothing to do with the miracle of his own raising, they wanted to kill Lazarus anyway. As you can see, the stage was definitely being set for what will happen on Good Friday.

So, why the triumphal entry? Why the rejoicing over the arrival of the One long ago promised? Why the need for a Messiah in the first place? Well, the Jews of the time would have told you one thing, while we see something else in the whole of Scripture. The Jews of the time were expecting a Messiah who they believed was promised to them to free them from the enslaving bonds of Roman rule. They viewed the promised Messiah's description of breaking the chains and freeing the people as referring to civil freedom. And while that will be an aspect of Christ's second coming, it was not, however, the ultimate purpose for His first.

The purpose for His first coming was to break the chains of sin, death, and hell which were reigning over all of us. We began this devotional study looking at what happened with Eve in the garden. We saw that she was deceived into eating the fruit God had commanded her not to eat. Beyond that, though, her husband, Adam, deliberately chose to disobey God and, in so doing, led to the passing down of a sin nature to each and every human being who would ever walk the earth.

In the midst of this darkness, this pain and separation from God as a result of sin, and this punishment that had to come in the form of death, even then our God shows Himself to be infinitely merciful and kind. In a similar circumstance where I as a parent would have been fed up, not even wanting to deal with my kids in that instant, our Heavenly Father behaved far differently. Even then He was already looking forward to a Messiah, a Redeemer Who would come and rescue His people from the bonds of sin. God never wanted to be eternally separated from us; He never wanted sin to come between Himself and His kids. And so He promised, all the way back then, on the very day sin first entered the world, a Savior.

We read of this Savior in Genesis 3:13-15,

> And the Lord God said to the woman, "What is this you have done?" The woman said, "The serpent deceived me, and I ate." So the Lord God said to the serpent: "Because you have done this, you are cursed more than all cattle, and more than every beast of the field; on your belly you shall go, and you shall eat dust all the days of your life. And I will put enmity between you and the woman, and between your seed and her Seed; He shall bruise your head, and you shall bruise His heel."

Salvation through Jesus our Messiah was no "Plan B" option God had to quickly come up with when Adam and Eve blew it. No, this was God's rescue plan for His children—a plan He had secured since before the dawn of time, since before sin ever even came into the world:

> Blessed be the God and Father of our Lord Jesus Christ, who has blessed us with every spiritual blessing in the heavenly *places*

in Christ, just as He chose us in Him before the foundation of the world, that we should be holy and without blame before Him in love, having predestined us to adoption as sons by Jesus Christ to Himself, according to the good pleasure of His will, to the praise of the glory of His grace, by which He made us accepted in the Beloved (Ephesians 1:3-6).

Before we ever needed a Messiah, God planned to provide us with one. And that is why there is so much to rejoice over on Palm Sunday.

Action Step:

Take a few minutes just to ponder the depths of what you have read here today. Before you ever sinned, before your parents ever sinned, before Adam and Eve ever sinned, God had already planned a way to rescue you from the bonds of the enemy. Our salvation does not come from our striving, but from the work Christ already accomplished on our behalf. Journal how that makes you feel and spend some time in worship.

Prayer:

Lord, thank You for this plan of rescue that You had all lined out before it was ever even needed. This realization shows me just how much I am loved and adored by You. You never wanted to have to be separated from me, so You made a way for me to come back to You. Help me to live in light of this realization, not just remembering it on Palm Sunday, but truly considering it and pondering it every day of the year. Thank You for Your grace and Your love. Help me to walk mindfully in them. In Jesus' name, Amen.

Day 35

Jesus' Rebuke of Unfaithful Living

Now the next day, when they had come out from Bethany, He was hungry. And seeing from afar a fig tree having leaves, He went to see if perhaps He would find something on it. When He came to it, He found nothing but leaves, for it was not the season for figs. In response Jesus said to it, "Let no one eat fruit from you ever again." And His disciples heard it. So they came to Jerusalem. Then Jesus went into the temple and began to drive out those who bought and sold in the temple, and overturned the tables of the money changers and the seats of those who sold doves. And He would not allow anyone to carry wares through the temple. Then He taught, saying to them, "Is it not written, 'My house shall be called a house of prayer for all nations'? But you have made it a 'den of thieves.'"....And Peter, remembering, said to Him, "Rabbi, look! The fig tree which You cursed has withered away." So Jesus answered and said to them, "Have faith in God."

—Mark 11:12-17, 21-22

Remember, O my soul, the fig tree was charged, not with bearing noxious fruit, but no fruit.

—Thomas Fuller[1]

The good news of the gospel is woven throughout much of what I write on my blog and in my books, as well as what I discuss on the podcast. I show women all the time how Paul's words in Romans 7

1 http://christian-quotes.ochristian.com/christian-quotes_ochristian.cgi?query=fig+tree&action=Search&x=0&y=0, accessed October 2, 2019

and 8 are the antidote for guilt, shame, and self-condemnation. I quote Psalm 103 often, reminding readers that the Lord "knows our frame; He remembers that we are dust" (verse 14). He knows we still have a sin nature we will have to fight against, and He knows that we will sometimes succumb to those temptations. Even so, Paul reminds us in Romans 8:1, "There is therefore now no condemnation to those who are in Christ Jesus." All of this is right and true, good to remember, and freeing to the soul.

But it is also just a portion of the whole story and picture of the Christian life. It isn't enough for us to simply delight in and relish God's amazing grace toward us and His freeing us from condemnation and guilt. We were never meant to simply remain in that place of only being thankful for the gospel. We were always intended to then walk out the implications of the gospel. We were designed to be sanctified more and more into the image of Christ. The Christian life begins with our experiencing immense gratitude for God's amazing grace, and then continues on into a life of increased obedience as a result of our gratitude.

This is not about legalism, mind you. Obedience and legalism are not the same thing. Legalism is an adherence to man-made rules, an embracing of not just true commands found in Scripture but also additional parameters added onto them by man. Legalism is about striving to be perfect in an effort to be approved of and accepted by God.

Obedience, on the other hand, stems from a freedom, a love, and a gratitude that comes from knowing you are already approved of and accepted by God as a result of the blood of Christ that covers you and the righteousness of Christ which is now your own. When you realize the depths of what God has done for you through Christ, that love and gratitude you feel is what then inspires your heart to want to live a life of obedience and producing good fruit.

Jesus was so infuriated with a fig tree with no figs because of how it pictures people who claim to follow God but bear no good fruit that is in keeping with repentance (see Matthew 3:8). This is likewise what angered Him in the temple. Here was the temple of God—a place of prayer and communing with the Father—being turned into a place of business. It wasn't that Jesus was against people earning money. It was that the way and method in which they were doing so was completely inappropriate. Not only were these people extortioners, charging folks for the animals they would need for sacrifice in the temple, but their doing so also kept the poor and destitute out on the fringe. The poor were financially and physically ostracized and marginalized in the temple as a result of these moneychangers and their booths. Jesus, ever one with a heart for the poor and the destitute, the downtrodden and the mistreated, was rightfully angered against these extortioners. Their actions were not at all begetting people who professed to follow God.

In keeping with what Jesus did to the fig tree and how He feels about us producing good fruit in our lives, John 15 is another most important passage to consider. In verses 1-8 Jesus says,

> "I am the true vine, and My Father is the vinedresser. Every branch in Me that does not bear fruit He takes away; and every branch that bears fruit He prunes, that it may bear more fruit. You are already clean because of the word which I have spoken to you. Abide in Me, and I in you. As the branch cannot bear fruit of itself, unless it abides in the vine, neither can you, unless you abide in Me. I am the vine, you *are* the branches. He who abides in Me, and I in him, bears much fruit; for without Me you can do nothing. If anyone does not abide in Me, he is cast out as a branch and is withered; and they gather them and throw *them* into the fire, and they are burned. If you abide in Me, and My words abide in you, you will ask what you desire, and it shall be done for you. By this My Father is glorified, that you bear much fruit; so you will be My disciples."

This is Christ's desire for us as His followers: that we would bear much fruit—fruit that is good for us and those around us—and bring glory to His name.

Action Step:

Assess how you are doing in the mission to abide in Christ. Abiding in Christ is referring to actions such as being in the Word, communing with Him in prayer, meditating on the good news of the gospel, and living in obedience to what He leads you to do. Abiding in Christ is not about striving; it is about resting in the Lord.

Prayer:

Lord, help me to have a heart that yearns to obey You. Not out of compulsion, not begrudgingly, or from the point of view of obedience equalling misery. Instead, help me to so live in light of Your grace, love, and mercy that I begin to view obedience more and more as a wonderful, freeing, positive thing. Grow me ever more into Your image. In Jesus' name, Amen.

Day 36

Jesus' and Our Priorities

And Jesus answered and spoke to them again by parables and said: "The kingdom of heaven is like a certain king who arranged a marriage for his son, and sent out his servants to call those who were invited to the wedding; and they were not willing to come. Again, he sent out other servants, saying, 'Tell those who are invited, See, I have prepared my dinner; my oxen and fatted cattle are killed, and all things are ready. Come to the wedding.' But they made light of it and went their ways, one to his own farm, another to his business. And the rest seized his servants, treated them spitefully, and killed them. But when the king heard about it, he was furious. And he sent out his armies, destroyed those murderers, and burned up their city. Then he said to his servants, 'The wedding is ready, but those who were invited were not worthy. Therefore go into the highways, and as many as you find, invite to the wedding.' So those servants went out into the highways and gathered together all whom they found, both bad and good. And the wedding hall was filled with guests."

—Matthew 22:1-10

The country people have their farms to look after, about which there is always something or other to do; the town's people must tend their shops, and be constant upon the exchange; they must buy, and sell, and get gain. It is true, that both farmers and merchants must be diligent in their business but not so as to keep them from making religion their main business. Licitis perimus omnes—These lawful things undo us, when they are unlawfully managed, when we are so careful and troubled about many things as to neglect the one thing needful. Observe, Both the city and the country have their temptations, the merchandise in the one, and the farms in the other; so that, whatever we have of the world in our hands, our care must be to keep it out of our hearts, lest it come between us and Christ.

—Matthew Henry[1]

Being a podcaster, blogger, author, and business owner, I operate in circles where it is very common for folks to talk about striving, hustling, and getting ahead. Making your dreams come true, pulling yourself up by your bootstraps, and taking courses designed to help you gain thousands of online followers are what is focused on by people in similar shoes to my own. The problem with this, however, is that it is all steeped in self-help rather than in the help and direction of the Holy Spirit.

The result is that priorities get out of whack, workaholism runs rampant, and the legitimately important tasks of work and ministry become idols which are raised up in the place of time spent with God and a focus on Him as our number one priority. When we forget this one thing that matters most—our day-in, day-out relationship with Him—we are in dangerous territory, just one step away from falling into the same trap into which Martha fell.

On the Tuesday of Holy Week, Jesus shared with His disciples a multitude of parables, answered questions regarding the resurrection, and discussed what is the greatest commandment. When trying to decide which of these many teachings to zero in on with you today, I felt compelled to choose this parable of the wedding. After all, Lent is that forty-day season wherein we seek to shut out the distractions of this world, cease our striving, and focus on the Lord. That is precisely what Jesus is teaching His followers to do in this passage from Matthew.

When we place anything ahead of our time with God, anything ahead of obeying Him, and anything higher on the list of those things which interest and delight us, we become guilty of idolatry. Sadly, that is precisely what is happening in this parable Jesus told.

Jesus tells the story of a king whose son was about to be married. It is said that in this parable, God the Father represents the king, Jesus represents the son, and He is marrying the church. As the wedding in the parable is being planned, the king's servants are sent out to invite

1 https://www.biblestudytools.com/commentaries/matthew-henry-complete/matthew/22.html, accessed October 2, 2019

people to come to the celebration and the subsequent feast that will follow. (Sounds like the marriage supper of the Lamb in Revelation, doesn't it?)

The problem, however, is that the people invited just don't see the wedding and the wedding feast as being all that big a deal. In fact, they "made light of it and went their ways, one to his own farm, another to his business." What did they view as being more important than the wedding celebration? Their homes and businesses.

How often do we behave this very same way? Sure, we may be professing believers and followers of Christ, but how often do we actually live as if that is a true description of us? How often do we seek the Lord in His Word and prayer? How often do we seek the guidance and direction of the Holy Spirit? On the flip side, how often do we spend time scrolling our phones, binge-watching Netflix, or working all hours of the day and night?

Sadly, this is a vicious cycle. The more we give in to our phones, our TVs, and our work, the less interesting prayer and Bible study seem to be in comparison. Then we crave our entertainment even more. And as the length of time increases between ourselves and the last time we were in the Word or prayer, the increasingly less likely we are to choose to turn to those practices.

As discouraging as that might sound, the opposite is also blessedly true. The more we choose to be in the Word and prayer (even if at first we don't feel like it), the more we will yearn for that communion with our Savior. We will find the Bible, replete with its stories of intrigue, danger, love, history, overthrown kingdoms, wisdom for the ages, and recipes for right living, come alive in an increasingly interesting way the more we pore over it. The more we pray, the more we will want to pray, wanting to always be in communication with our God throughout the day.

Truly, the key to us not growing lackadaisical or complacent in our view of the glorious good news of the gospel is choosing to live in light of it, choosing to be in the Word and in prayer, and choosing to walk by the Spirit—even when we don't feel like it.

Action Step:

Hustle, hurry, and over-scheduling are the enemies of an ever-growing relationship with the Lord and appreciation for His gospel. Take out your calendar and mark off two things that are not truly necessary or beneficial. Take out your to-do list for this week and do the same thing. Fill that newly-discovered free time with time spent with the Lord. Then, watch your relationship grow and deepen as a result!

Prayer:

Lord, You know how easily distracted I am. I love my work, want to get ahead, want to accomplish great things. Then I need to unwind at the end of a busy day, and You know how often I turn solely to entertainment for that. But, in the midst of activities that might be great and which might be a blessing to my family, help me not to lose sight of the true goal, the one thing that will be a blessing to myself and my family more than anything else: spending time with You. Help me to remember the truth of what Paul says in 2 Timothy 3:16-17—that it is the Word which equips me for every good work in this life. This Lenten season, help me to cease my striving in areas that are unimportant and instead focus on the truly most important things, knowing that everything else will flow from there, just as Jesus taught in Matthew 6:33. In Jesus' name, Amen.

Day 31

The Betrayal of Jesus

Now it came to pass, when Jesus had finished all these sayings, that He said to His disciples, "You know that after two days is the Passover, and the Son of Man will be delivered up to be crucified." Then the chief priests, the scribes, and the elders of the people assembled at the palace of the high priest, who was called Caiaphas, and plotted to take Jesus by trickery and kill Him. But they said, "Not during the feast, lest there be an uproar among the people."…..Then one of the twelve, called Judas Iscariot, went to the chief priests and said, "What are you willing to give me if I deliver Him to you?" And they counted out to him thirty pieces of silver. So from that time he sought opportunity to betray Him.

—Matthew 26:1-5, 15-16

The Christian will be sure to make enemies. It will be one of his objects to make none; but if doing what is right and believing what is true should cause him to lose every earthly friend, he will regard it as a small loss, since his great Friend in heaven will be even more friendly and will reveal Himself to him more graciously than ever.

—Alistair Begg[1]

It never ceases to amaze me that Jesus intentionally chose Judas Iscariot to be one of His disciples during His earthly ministry, when He knew full well that the day would come in which Judas would betray Him. And we aren't even just talking here about a betrayal like that of which Peter was guilty—that of telling someone he wasn't Christ's disciple when, in reality, he had been. No, this was a betrayal of mammoth proportions, a betrayal that would lead not only to Jesus' capture and arrest, but ultimately to His death.

Imagine the gut-wrenching depth of a betrayal like this one. Here was someone whom you had chosen to be a part of your community and your mission, someone with whom you had truly done life for three years. And what happens? He not only betrays you and betrays you in a way that leads to your death, but he does so in a sarcastic, snide, and humiliating way. We read of this in Matthew 26:47-56:

> And while He was still speaking, behold, Judas, one of the twelve, with a great multitude with swords and clubs, came from the chief priests and elders of the people. Now His betrayer had given them a sign, saying, "Whomever I kiss, He is the One; seize Him." Immediately he went up to Jesus and said, "Greetings, Rabbi!" and kissed Him. But Jesus said to him, "Friend, why have you come?" Then they came and laid hands on Jesus and took Him. And suddenly, one of those *who were* with Jesus stretched out *his* hand and drew his sword, struck the servant of the high priest, and cut off his ear. But Jesus said to him, "Put your sword in its place, for all who take the sword will perish by the sword. Or do you think that I cannot now pray to My Father, and He will provide Me with more than twelve legions of angels? How then could the Scriptures be fulfilled, that it must happen thus?" In that hour Jesus said to the multitudes, "Have you come out, as against a robber, with swords and clubs to take Me? I sat daily with you, teaching in the temple, and you did not seize Me. But all this was done that the Scriptures of the prophets might be fulfilled." Then all the disciples forsook Him and fled.

Can you imagine going through something like that? Can you imagine the depth of pain and loss, the sense of betrayal, the feeling that these men with whom you had journeyed through life so closely for the last few years are actually acting as nothing more than fair-weather friends—and one of them truly is? It's unfathomable. And yet, it is precisely what Jesus experienced in order to fulfill the Scriptures and obtain our salvation. That, my friend, is how much He loves you and is willing to experience for your sake!

I don't know if you have ever experienced the betrayal of a friend or other loved one, but if you have, chances are you have been tempted to strive for perfection, to bend over backward to do anything you possibly can to win them back, to please them, to make everything okay. Or perhaps your striving has taken on a different form. You have been striving to forget about them, striving to hold bitterness in your heart so that you don't even have to think about possibly forgiving them. You have been striving to journey through life without them or at least without the pain that regularly surfaces when you think about them.

This Lenten season, may I encourage you to cease your striving in this area as well? If you are busy looking for the answer to your problems within your own bitterness or within your own "perfection," may I encourage you to lay that all down at the feet of Jesus and be freed from those feelings and that striving once and for all? Jesus wants rest, freedom, an easy yoke, and a light burden for you (see Matthew 11:28-30). And He knows that will only come from your doing life His way.

If your struggle is one of striving for perfection, there are several helpful passages for you. One would be Philippians 3:4b-11:

> If anyone else thinks he may have confidence in the flesh, I more so: circumcised the eighth day, of the stock of Israel, *of* the tribe of Benjamin, a Hebrew of the Hebrews; concerning the law, a Pharisee; concerning zeal, persecuting the church; concerning the righteousness which is in the law, blameless. But what things were gain to me, these I have counted loss for Christ. Yet indeed I also count all things loss for the excellence of the knowledge of Christ Jesus my Lord, for whom I have suffered the loss of all things, and count them as rubbish, that I may gain Christ and be found in Him, not having my own righteousness, which *is* from the law, but that which *is* through faith in Christ, the righteousness which is from God by faith; that I may know Him and the power of His resurrection, and the fellowship of His sufferings, being conformed to His death, if, by any means, I may attain to the resurrection from the dead.

Your striving for perfection is worthless and not that to which God has called you. If that is your response to someone's betrayal, it's time to let it go.

Conversely, if you struggle with a lack of forgiveness, Romans 12:19-21 is for you:

> Beloved, do not avenge yourselves, but *rather* give place to wrath; for it is written, "Vengeance is Mine, I will repay," says the Lord. Therefore "If your enemy is hungry, feed him; If he is thirsty, give him a drink; For in so doing you will heap coals of fire on his head." Do not be overcome by evil, but overcome evil with good.

Matthew 6:14-15 is another to consider:

> For if you forgive men their trespasses, your heavenly Father will also forgive you. But if you do not forgive men their trespasses, neither will your Father forgive your trespasses.

This may seem to be an impossible mission, but if you purpose in your heart to forgive the one who has betrayed you, you will have strength through Christ and His gift of the Holy Spirit to walk that path of grace and forgiveness as He has called you to do. You are never alone in your mission to do what's right.

Action Step:

Search your heart and see if there is any unresolved betrayal in your past. Is there someone whose approval you are striving to earn? Is there someone you are unwilling to forgive? Ask the Lord to help you in whatever way you need as you seek to be free from this bondage of striving.

Prayer:

Lord, You know firsthand how much it hurts to be betrayed, abandoned, and rejected by those close to You, especially in Your hour of need. Help me to find comfort in that, knowing I am not alone in my pain and in my struggles. Please bring good out of this situation, and help me to live through it in a way that is honoring to You. Thank You that I have You to lean on. In Jesus' name, Amen.

Day 38

Jesus' Preparation and Hospitality for Us

Now on the first day of the Feast of the Unleavened Bread the disciples came to Jesus, saying to Him, "Where do You want us to prepare for You to eat the Passover?" And He said, "Go into the city to a certain man, and say to him, 'The Teacher says, "My time is at hand; I will keep the Passover at your house with My disciples."'" So the disciples did as Jesus had directed them; and they prepared the Passover. When evening had come, He sat down with the twelve. Now as they were eating, He said, "Assuredly, I say to you, one of you will betray Me." And they were exceedingly sorrowful, and each of them began to say to Him, "Lord, is it I?" He answered and said, "He who dipped his hand with Me in the dish will betray Me. The Son of Man indeed goes just as it is written of Him, but woe to that man by whom the Son of Man is betrayed! It would have been good for that man if he had not been born." Then Judas, who was betraying Him, answered and said, "Rabbi, is it I?" He said to him, "You have said it." And as they were eating, Jesus took bread, blessed and broke it, and gave it to the disciples and said, "Take, eat; this is My body." Then He took the cup, and gave thanks, and gave it to them, saying, "Drink from it, all of you. For this is My blood of the new covenant, which is shed for many for the remission of sins. But I say to you, I will not drink of this fruit of the vine from now on until that day when I drink it new with you in My Father's kingdom." And when they had sung a hymn, they went out to the Mount of Olives.

—Matthew 26:17-30

The Christian community is a community of the cross, for it has been brought into being by the cross, and the focus of its worship is the Lamb once slain, now glorified. So the community of the cross is a community of celebration, a eucharistic community, ceaselessly offering to God through Christ the sacrifice of our praise and thanksgiving. The Christian life is an unending festival. And the festival we keep, now that our Passover Lamb has been sacrificed for us, is a joyful celebration of his sacrifice, together with a spiritual feasting upon it.

—John Stott[1]

I love the scene we are given in this passage from Matthew 26. Here, at a time when Jesus is now only a day away from being crucified—killed in a most horrible and excruciating manner—we see the tender heart He had for His people. Knowing full well what lies ahead of Him and the pain and heartache He will endure, He nevertheless shifts His focus to His disciples. The time has come for the Passover meal, and Jesus has already, ahead of time, prepared specifically where it is that their group of friends will share the meal. He has been proactive to prepare a place for them, thinking of their needs and operating out of a place of forethought, preparation, and hospitality.

With all that is coming for Jesus the next day, He takes the time to slow down, to gather in close with His disciples, and celebrate this important feast in an intimate and special way. This is what has become known as the Last Supper, and it is on this day that Jesus instituted what we know now and commemorate as the Eucharist or Lord's Supper. Jesus takes this time to commune with His disciples, to break bread with them, to share wine, and to encourage and prepare their hearts, in both word and song, for what lies ahead.

Truly, this is not just any meal. This encounter is one of more than just breaking bread and drinking wine and fellowshipping as friends. This is a conversation, a passage from Scripture, that is most rich in its doctrine and theology. Over dinner, Jesus speaks on subjects pertaining to the New Covenant, the remission of our sins, and even eschatology—the "doctrine of the last things."

---

1 http://christian-quotes.ochristian.com/christian-quotes_ochristian.cgi?query=passover&action=Search&x=0&y=0, accessed October 3, 2019

In this passage, Jesus presents to us the best example we have, a first-hand picture, for how to practice hospitality. Jesus does not rush around and strive; He does not overwhelm or stress Himself with the preparations. Instead, He begins them well ahead of time, setting everything in motion early so that everything will come together when it is time for dinner and guests and fellowship.

Once His guests arrive, His focus is on them. He is interested in meeting their physical needs through food and their spiritual needs through doctrine, theology, and spiritual practices. He meets their mental and emotional needs by letting them know ahead of time a little bit about what would transpire, while also encouraging and supporting them in and through it. Talk about an example!

As believers, we know that we have been tasked with the mission and ministry of hospitality. We are told, unequivocally, that we are to be hospitable and not to forsake the extending of hospitality. But too often, we hit a wall in this area because we act a little too much like Jesus' friend Martha. We begin with our service rather than our relationship with the Lord. We rush ahead of time spent with Jesus to instead focus on our to-do list of tasks we feel we must accomplish before our guests arrive. Then, we begin to disdain service and hospitality because of all the stress and overwhelm it seems to bring us.

The answer to this age-old struggle is to begin as did Mary—to be at the feet of Jesus, communing with and learning from Him. Starting off on that right foot will lead to a most enjoyable, fruitful, kingdom-impacting ministry of hospitality. May we heed Jesus' example, rather than continuing on in our own predisposition to strive, and have all our lives changed for the better as we do!

Action Step:

Compare how you usually prepare for a time of hospitality to how Jesus prepared in this passage. Compare the feel of the conversation and atmosphere during your times of hospitality to that of Jesus with His disciples. Take a minute to consider what might need to change.

Prayer:

Lord, thank You for the beautiful example You give in this passage of how to love on, serve, and teach others over the table. Thank You for what it reveals about Your tender heart for Your people. Help me to live out this example to all those who come into my home—friends, family, and strangers alike. Help me to point them to You and Your love in all I do. In Jesus' name, Amen.

Day 39

The Worst Good Day

When Pilate heard these words, he brought Jesus outside. He sat down on the judge's seat in a place called the Stone Pavement (but in Aramaic, Gabbatha). It was the preparation day for the Passover, and it was about noon. Then he told the Jews, "Here is your king!" They shouted, "Take him away! Take him away! Crucify him!" Pilate said to them, "Should I crucify your king?" "We have no king but Caesar!" the chief priests answered. Then he handed him over to be crucified.

—John 19:13-16

We may say that on the first Good Friday afternoon was completed that great act by which light conquered darkness and goodness conquered sin. That is the wonder of our Saviour's crucifixion. There have been victories all over the world, but wherever we look for the victor we expect to find him with his heel upon the neck of the vanquished. The wonder of Good Friday is that the victor lies vanquished by the vanquished one. We have to look deeper into the very heart and essence of things before we can see how real the victory is that thus hides under the guise of defeat.

—Phillips Brooks[1]

The day had come. After three years of public ministry and one last very eventful week, the moment had come for Jesus to give up His

1 https://www.thoughtco.com/good-friday-quotes-2832521, accessed December 19, 2019

life. What we celebrate at Christmastime with gifts, festivities, and great joy—the birth of the Messiah—had all led up to this. But the feel is different than that of Christmas morning. We don't sing songs on this day that has commonly become known as "Good Friday." We don't exchange gifts, admire special decorations, or speak of "good tidings of great joy." Truly, the day just doesn't really feel all that good.

Especially when you read the account of all that happened to Jesus on this so-called good day.

But that is precisely what we have to remember—this was (and is) truly a good day! As we read the full account of all that Christ endured on this day, we are horrified—and rightfully so. It's barbaric, it's tortuous, it's bloody. But what it led to, what it resulted in, is what caused it to be a good day.

On Good Friday this year, nearly two thousand years removed, we can stop, look back, ponder, and believe it was, in fact, a good day. Because it is the very day the Lord secured freedom, salvation, hope, and eternal life for us, all at once. As Jesus said in His final moment of life while on the cross, "It is finished." (See John 19:30.)

All those things we have seen women of the Bible yearn for and strive to find—all those very same things we are on a quest for ourselves—can be and are fulfilled in Christ as a result of what He secured for us on the cross:

• He secured salvation for us—no longer do we have to be on a quest to try to earn acceptance and eternal life.

• He secured an identity for us—no longer do we have to wonder who we are or seek to "discover" ourselves.

• He secured a purpose for us—no longer do we have to wonder why we were born or strive for impact in our everyday lives.

• He secured love for us—no longer do we have to strive to earn love or despair over our seeming lack of it.

• He secured an eternal family for us—no longer do we have to strive for relationships.

• He secured fulfillment for us—no longer do we have to strive to look for someone or something who will fill us up.

- He secured rest for us—no longer do we have to work ourselves to the bone as if we are employees of God; we can rest in His grace as beloved children of God.

All of this—every single last thing we have talked about in this Lenten study thus far—and more was secured for us on the cross on that very good Friday all those years ago. If it weren't for what happened on Good Friday, we would not be able to find in Christ the fulfillment we long for in each of these areas. That, my friend, is why we are able to call such a dark, sad, anguish-filled day "good." May that serve as a daily reminder for you of how God can and does bring immense good out of everything. He did it then, and He is still doing it today.

Action Step:

Read through all of John 19 and Isaiah 53 to fully grasp and understand all that Jesus went through and willingly endured out of immense and deep love for you. Meditate on the implications of His love.

Prayer:

Lord, it is absolutely horrific all that You endured on my behalf on the cross. You endured the shame, pain, torture, and ridicule so willingly—and all for me—so that I might always live with You. Thank You for this love. I can't even fathom it, but I thank You that it is mine. Help me to walk the rest of my life in light of Your love for me. Help me to find my joy, my purpose, my fulfillment, and my identity in this love. And may it make a difference in how I love others. In Jesus' name, Amen.

Day 40

When All Hope Seems Lost

It was the preparation day, and the Sabbath was about to begin. The women who had come with him from Galilee followed along and observed the tomb and how his body was placed. Then they returned and prepared spices and perfumes. And they rested on the Sabbath according to the commandment.

—Luke 23:54-56

We say, then, to anyone who is under trial, give Him time to steep the soul in His eternal truth. Go into the open air, look up into the depths of the sky, or out upon the wideness of the sea, or on the strength of the hills that is His also; or, if bound in the body, go forth in the spirit; spirit is not bound. Give Him time and, as surely as dawn follows night, there will break upon the heart a sense of certainty that cannot be shaken.

—Amy Carmichael[1]

I can't imagine how the followers of Christ must have felt on that Saturday, that dark day after the crucifixion and before the resurrection. It was a dark in-between day. The gruesome scene of Calvary was behind them, but the joy of Easter was as yet nowhere to be found. All they had were their memories of the past and their not-yet-fulfilled promises of the future.

---

1 http://christian-quotes.ochristian.com/christian-quotes_ochristian.cgi?query=trial&action=Search&x=0&y=0, accessed December 4, 2019

Perhaps you can relate. It could be that even as you read these words you are in a dark in between of your own. Something has happened in your life, and the joys of yesterday are nowhere to be found. Far away, too, are the promises of tomorrow.

You remember the days of long ago when it felt so easy to believe in God's faithfulness, in His trustworthy nature, in His love. You hadn't yet endured any hard trials, you hadn't yet borne the brunt of heartache and pain, and the darkness of this fallen world had not yet touched you in any real life-altering way.

But now it has. And the pain cuts incredibly deep into the inner core of your soul itself.

Now everything is different. Now it isn't quite so easy to just conjure up the Bible verses you memorized in Sunday school and feel the instant comfort and hope they used to bring. Now when you think of the promises of Scripture, you feel as if they are almost mocking you, dangling the carrot of hope and good news in front of you, but with no hope for your ability to reach out and grasp them for yourself.

That is quite likely exactly how the disciples were feeling on the Saturday of Holy Week. And, as it turns out, they weren't the only ones. Years and years before, the Israelites had felt that very same in-between feeling, that same struggle to hold on to hope when all hope seemed to be lost.

We're all likely familiar with the promise of Jeremiah 29:11; after all, we see it printed everywhere we turn:

> "For I know the plans I have for you"—this is the Lord's declaration—"plans for your well-being, not for disaster, to give you a future and a hope."

But what you may not realize is that at the time in which this promise was proclaimed to God's people, they were in their own hard and dark in-between season.

Gone were the days of enjoying the promised land of milk and honey. They were now embarking on seventy years of captivity in the land of Babylon. That is the dark season in which they find themselves when God utters this promise to them.

Somewhere during those long seventy years (much lengthier than one twenty-four hour Saturday!), God's promise must have felt like nothing more than a bunch of empty words all strung together. But they learned what we, too, must remember to be true: "The Lord does not delay his promise, as some understand delay" (see 2 Peter 3:9).

God always fulfills His promises, and there is always a reason for the precise timing in which He chooses to do so. It's not an easy road to walk, this in-between season of darkness. But it will not last forever. It will not go on indefinitely. Resurrection is right around the corner.

Action Step:

Do a mini Bible study of the life of Joseph as outlined in Genesis 38-50. Make a list of all the dark hardships and trials he endured, and then make a list of the reasons God gave for those very heartaches. Cling to the faithfulness of God in your own situation.

Prayer:

Lord, I'm stuck in the dark in between. I'm finding it hard to cling to hope. I'm finding it hard, as the disciples must have, to remember and believe and hold fast to Your promises. They seem so far off, so elusive. But I know that with You, all Your promises will be fulfilled, and joy will come again. Help me to cling to that fact. Help me to hold on for resurrection morning. In Jesus' name, Amen.

In Conclusion
Easter Sunday: As We Go

But Mary stood outside the tomb, crying. As she was crying, she stooped to look into the tomb. She saw two angels in white sitting where Jesus's body had been lying, one at the head and the other at the feet. They said to her, "Woman, why are you crying?" "Because they've taken away my Lord," she told them, "and I don't know where they've put him." Having said this, she turned around and saw Jesus standing there, but she did not know it was Jesus. "Woman," Jesus said to her, "why are you crying? Who is it that you're seeking?" Supposing he was the gardener, she replied, "Sir, if you've carried him away, tell me where you've put him, and I will take him away." Jesus said to her, "Mary." Turning around, she said to him in Aramaic, "Rabboni!"—which means "Teacher." "Don't cling to me," Jesus told her, "since I have not yet ascended to the Father. But go to my brothers and tell them that I am ascending to my Father and your Father, to my God and your God." Mary Magdalene went and announced to the disciples, "I have seen the Lord!" And she told them what he had said to her.

—John 20:11-18

Receive every day as a resurrection from death, as a new enjoyment of life; meet every rising sun with such sentiments of God's goodness, as if you had seen it, and all things, new-created upon your account: and under the sense of so great a blessing, let your joyful heart praise and magnify so good and glorious a Creator.

—William Law[1]

1 http://christian-quotes.ochristian.com/christian-quotes_ochristian.cgi?query=resurrection&action=Search&x=0&y=0, accessed December 19, 2019

Theologian Thomas Fuller once said, "It is always darkest just before the day dawneth."[2] How very true in the case of Holy Week! Imagine being in the shoes of the disciples, grieving the loss of your beloved Teacher and Friend. You have seen Him brutally killed, and you have lived through a whole day without Him. You're feeling more than a little discombobulated. For three years, you have done life with Him—travelled with Him, left behind jobs and family for Him, lodged with Him, eaten with Him, learned from Him, and watched Him perform amazing miracles. Now, all of a sudden, you are alone. He is nowhere in sight, and you aren't quite sure what to do with yourself. As if the confusion weren't enough, the grief itself threatens to undo you.

And then. And then came bursting forth the glorious good news, a brand new kind of good tidings of glad joy on that life-changing Sunday morning!

If you have followed along with any of my writings for very long, you know how much I delight in pointing out our tender Savior's view and treatment of women. I've said before that in a culture which degraded women and put them down, Christ raised them up. We see that so vividly and strikingly here in this resurrection passage.

What we must understand is that in the Jewish culture of the time, a woman's witness was worth about half that of a man's. In a court of law, two female witnesses were required for every male witness. Women were thought to be deceivers, liars, brainless, and dangerous. With that in mind, it becomes even more amazing to see that it was to a woman that Jesus first appeared following His resurrection! And not only that, but He tasked a woman with the mission of proclaiming the fact of the resurrection to the other disciples!

On that beautiful Easter morning, it was Mary Magdalene who travelled to the tomb. And it was Mary Magdalene who first saw the risen Lord. What a tender and astonishing moment. One that undoubtedly changed her life forever!

On this very morning (or evening!) as you read these words, let the very same joy, astonishment, wonder, and hope fill your heart and mind anew as it did Mary Magdalene's. Ponder on these things as if you have never read the resurrection story before. Let that joy sink deep down into your heart after what may have been a trying season of Lent for you.

---

2 https://www.answers.com/Q/Who_said_the_night_is_always_darkest_just_before_the_dawn, accessed December 19, 2019

Realize that it is Jesus' resurrection that secures your own resurrection. Remember that it is His rising from the dead that secures your eternal life. And now, as we go on from here, walk forward in that sense of joy and thanksgiving every day of your life on this earth. Allow it to change how you think, speak, act, and live out the moments of your ordinary life. Make Mary Magdalene's task your own, and go forth in glad tidings of great joy, sharing with others about the reason for the hope, joy, and love that is within you. You can officially cease your striving, friend. And Resurrection Sunday is why.

Action Step:

Read Matthew 20:18-20. This is your life's mission statement in light of the resurrection. How will you allow that truth to change your daily life from this very moment until you see your Savior face to face? Journal your thoughts.

Prayer:

Lord, the joy that wells up from within my heart at the thought of Your resurrection on that beautiful Sunday morning all those years ago is almost more than I can put into words! You vanquished hell, sin, death, and the grave. You conquered it all, and I can walk forth in new life now and in eternity as a result. Thank You, Lord! Thank You for the good news of this day. May I walk in light of this joy and good news every day of my life and, by Your grace, inspire others to do the same. In Jesus' name, Amen.

About the Author

Rebekah Hargraves is a wife, homeschooling mama of two littles, author, podcaster, and blogger whose passion is to see women living in light of the gospel and learning to walk by the Spirit in their everyday lives. To that end, she hosts the Home and Hearth podcast, runs the Hargraves Home and Hearth blog, and contributes to many other sites online including Project Inspired, Her View from Home, The Christian Post, and Thrive Moms.

She delights in hearing from her readers, so if you have enjoyed this Lenten devotional, please do reach out to her through her website (HargravesHomeandHearth.com) or on Instagram (@rebekahhargraves) or Facebook (Hargraves Home and Hearth). Let her know what stood out to you the most from your study time this Lent!

Made in the USA
Monee, IL
27 February 2023

28785113R00113